CW00520675

T_ _
Anxiety-Filled
Diary of a
Pregnant
Hypochondriac

By Amber McNaught

ISBN 9781687670830
2020 Edition

ACKNOWLEDGEMENTS

This book would not exist without the support of my long-suffering husband and parents, who have always been there for me, through good times and bad, so my thanks, as always go first of all to them, and would take another book for me to list in detail.

This book would also not exist, however, without the wonderful NHS staff, who were there to support me through miscarriage and ectopic pregnancy, all the way through to childbirth. We're extremely fortunate in the UK to have access to some of the best quality medical care in the world, and I was able to experience that first hand: I could not have asked for better care, but, just as importantly, I could not have asked for more kindness and understanding than was shown to me over the course of the two years it took to create our Max.

I went into pregnancy with an extreme phobia of hospitals and childbirth, and while my experience didn't exactly cure me, I was absolutely blown away by the level of non-judgemental support I was given by the medical staff I encountered. My thanks go in particular to:

- Jill, at the Early Pregnancy Unit, St. John's Hospital, Livingston, without whose kindness and encouragement I would almost certainly have given up after my first two failed experiences of pregnancy. Thank you for staying late to call me with the results of my blood test, and for assuring me repeatedly that I wasn't crazy to try again.

- Julie, the sonographer who did all of my first scans, and who was almost as happy as we were to see the tiny dot that was to become Max on the screen. Thank you for understanding my fears, and for making sure my scans were allocated to you, so you could help me through them.

- Carolyn, the wonderful midwife who was there for us both from my very first appointment, right up until Max came home from hospital. Thank you for patiently answering my questions, allaying my fears, and doing everything in your power to do exactly what you said you would: make sure Max got here in the safest, and least traumatic way possible.

Finally, this book is dedicated to my lovely mother-in-law, Soula, who may not be here to read it, but who is always in our hearts.

INTRODUCTION

On December 29th, 2017, I gave birth to my baby son, Max, by elective c-section.

It would be wrong, of course, to describe Max's birth as a miracle: babies are born every day, after all (A quick Google search tells me at least 200 will have entered the world in the time it's taken me to write this sentence...), and there's absolutely nothing "miraculous" about it. For me, though, it really did feel like one: purely because the journey to get there - to that operating theatre, on a snowy December day - had been so very hard. I, you see, suffer from tokophobia: which is loosely defined as a fear of pregnancy and childbirth. Tokophobia affects different people in different ways, but, in my case, my fears were so great that, up until a few years ago, I had gone through my entire life determined to never, ever get pregnant: because, if I did, I was sure it would kill me.

Well, spoiler alert: it did not kill me. I guess that much is pretty obvious, huh?

There were times, however, when I really felt like it was going to: kill me, I mean. Like when my first pregnancy ended in miscarriage at 6 weeks, for instance. Or when the second, just two months later, turned out to be ectopic. Both of those things were aspects of pregnancy that I'd worried about obsessively - particularly the ectopic, which was one of my biggest fears. When those fears actually came true, they served purely to validate my belief that pregnancy was risky and terrifying: that it could, quite literally, kill me, and that it was something to be avoided at all costs.

I didn't avoid it at all costs, though.

No, instead, my husband, Terry and I, decided to give it one last try, and, in May 2017, we found out that I was pregnant for the third time.

This time, I decided to write about it.

At that point, my blog, ForeverAmber.co.uk, had been online for over 11 years, serving primarily as an online diary and record of my life. I'd been keeping diaries since I was a little girl, and my blog was a natural extension of that - and of my work as a journalist. More importantly, though, the community of readers I'd built up over the years I'd been blogging had become a huge source of support and comfort to me. They'd been there for me during the dark days of my ectopic pregnancy, and through all of the various other landmark moments in my life, and I knew they'd be there for me now, as I embarked upon my third pregnancy, without a single hope of it actually working out.

So I started to keep a pregnancy diary: first of all in an old notebook I dug out of a desk drawer right after my miscarriage, and then on the blog itself, once we got to 12 weeks, and decided to go public.

Right from the very start, I knew I wanted my pregnancy diary to be an honest one: to tell the truth about pregnancy - or MY truth, at least - without sugarcoating it, or pretending to be finding it easy. It's not that I wasn't grateful to be pregnant: after two losses, I knew exactly how lucky I was to finally be experiencing what seemed to be a healthy pregnancy. It's just that, pregnancy after loss, or when you suffer from tokophobia/anxiety (In addition to my fear of childbirth, I also have a crippling phobia of general anaesthetics, and hospitals in general. Add in a bad case of health anxiety, and, well, you're probably getting close to understanding why pregnancy was such a scary time for me...) is very different from "normal" pregnancy. It's a time when you can't allow yourself to hope things will work out, and when every single trip to the bathroom becomes an exercise in terror, as you wait for a sign that something is wrong.

It's the kind of experience, in other words, that I think only those who've experienced pregnancy loss or pregnancy-related anxiety, can really understand: and, luckily for me, by writing openly and honestly about my experience, I found plenty of people who *did.*

As the weeks went on, and my pregnancy progressed, something unexpected started to happen. Instead of the disapproving comments and reminders to "Just be positive!" that I'd expected my honest thoughts about pregnancy to generate, I started to get emails and messages of solidarity and thanks. I'd thought people would think I was crazy for being so terrified, or would admonish me for not appearing appropriately grateful: actually, though, the opposite turned out to be true.

Sure, there were a few people who didn't get it: ones who felt I just wasn't trying hard enough to stop worrying, or who believed a quick spot of retail therapy (Or, more often, yoga. God, I hate yoga...) would easily cure a mental health issue I'd been dealing with for my entire adult life. If only it were that simple, right?

For the most part, though, people understood: and, not just that, they REALLY understood.

In the two years that have now passed since I started writing my pregnancy diary, I've received dozens - maybe even hundreds - of messages from women who feel the same. Women who've gone through pregnancy loss, or who are dealing with tokophobia: even ones who haven't experienced any of those things, but who are, nevertheless, still anxious about their pregnancies, and desperate to know they're not the only ones who feel that way.

This book is for those women.

Despite the diary format, this isn't a week-by-week guide to pregnancy. You won't find any medical information, product recommendations, or graphics showing you which fruit your baby most resembles this week: it's not that kind of diary. Instead, you'll find a very personal account of what it's like to go through pregnancy when every single moment seems to bring you something else to worry about, and when you feel like the only person in the world who feels that way.

Well, you're not: and, by sharing my story, my hope is to do for other women what they did for me when I first started writing about my pregnancy - to help them feel a little bit less alone, and maybe even give them a bit of hope that it *is* possible to survive pregnancy, even when you're scared to death.
After all, if I can do it, anyone can.

BEFORE
30/8/16

After the miscarriage was confirmed, we went to McDonald's.

It was a beautiful, blue-sky day: and in that other world - the one that ended so abruptly last Saturday afternoon - we'd probably have gone for a drive somewhere picturesque, and I'd have commented on how lucky we were to be having such a lovely, late summer; feeling almost as if this pregnancy heralded a fresh, new start, in which the sky would always be blue, and it would always be summer. But sunshine is not just for happy days. It was shining, for instance, when I emerged from that dark, curtained-off basement cubicle, in which two kind-faced women had broken the news I already knew, and I'd found myself trying to reassure *them*, rather than the other way around.

"Oh, it's OK," I'd said quickly, as they leaned over the bed, their faces carefully solemn. "It's OK: I already knew."

But it wasn't OK. And as I shuffled into that sunlit booth at McDonald's, a little while later, I was suddenly blindsided by a feeling of NOT OK.

It was Not OK to be sitting here eating a cheeseburger and fries when my baby was dead. It was Not OK for the sun to be shining, as if nothing had changed. Nothing was OK any more.

But the world was still rudely going about its business, and I hadn't eaten for over 24 hours, so although I still didn't really *want* to eat, fast food seemed like the easiest solution. If nothing else, it would get my parents and Terry off my back - sometimes the path of least resistance is the only one open to you.

The restaurant was sunny and frantic, the day more surreal

than any I can recall. As I sat there, I was reminded ...

(Short pause here, as Terry appears, bringing coffee and the mail. Mail which turns out to be the pack of 'Poorly Pouches' - sick bags - I'd ordered online just a few days ago, thinking that morning sickness would surely kick in any time now. I wonder how many more of these cruel reminders are in the post - in this case, quite literally? I wonder if it's normal to cry over a pack of 12 sick bags?)

As I sat there in my booth in that restaurant, I was reminded of the last time I ate in a fast-food chain: Burger King, in Tenerife, on the last day of our holiday, back in March. We were on the way to the airport, and I sat at our outdoor table with the suitcases crammed awkwardly underneath it, while Terry queued for food, which he immediately dropped down his brand new shirt.

That was a different world, though: the one where I hadn't even decided whether or not I really wanted a baby, anyway. Now, just five months later, I'm sitting in bed, still going through the miscarriage that 5-months-ago-me would not even have believed possible, and crying over an envelope I opened to reveal 12 paper bags, all in a row.

That other me, that *5-months-ago-me*, would not have recognised the person I am now. I've changed twice since then. I have been three different people in the space of a year. I wonder how many other people have that particular claim to fame? I wonder how many more of us are out there?

The First Me

The first me lived for almost 39 years. She did not ever want to have children: she was too much *herself* for that. She was sure she was much more *her*self than other people were *themselves* - and although she didn't particularly like the self she was, it was the only self she knew, and she didn't want to change.

Having a baby would do that: she knew it, had seen it. Having a baby would mean losing herself altogether - and that was a tragedy that could not be borne.

She did not want to become 'Baby's Mummy', as she'd seen other women become. Sometimes it was something those women even welcomed - encouraged, even. They changed their Facebook names to 'Callum's Mummy' - or whatever their child's name was - and that was how they defined themselves. They were mothers - or 'mamas', as the trend is now - and nothing else about them mattered anymore.

Sometimes, however, this loss of identity was thrust upon these new mothers, whether they wanted it or not. I'd seen it in the comments sections of the fashion blogs I read. 'Looking good, mama!' people would say on the page of someone who'd only written about her new dress, making absolutely no mention of her status as a mother, but being defined by it anyway - *other people* deciding it was the only thing that mattered.
"After I had you," my own mother told me once, "I noticed that people stopped using my name: in fact, some of them didn't even know it. I was always 'Amber's Mummy' after that, and it took a bit of getting used to."

My mum had wanted me so much that she'd been willing to try again after her own miscarriage, but still she was wrong-footed by the sudden switch to 'Amber's Mummy' from the person she'd been before. How would *I* manage it, then: especially when the very thought of having a baby terrified me half to death?

I had always been afraid of getting pregnant: and if you were to ask me why, my answer would most likely be, "Why not?" I mean, we're talking about a scenario here in which an *entire person* grows inside another person's body, and then has to be pushed out amid scenes that wouldn't be even remotely out of place in a horror movie. Who *wouldn't* be scared of that? The fact was, I wasn't just scared *to* death: I was scared *of* death - and it seemed to me that pregnancy and childbirth provided women with so many different opportunities to die.

You could have a miscarriage, and have to have an operation to remove it. It was called a D&C, and, from what I'd heard, it seemed to involve a general anaesthetic, which was - and IS - one of my biggest fears.

You could have an ectopic pregnancy, which ruptured and killed you.

You could have a post-partum haemorrhage. Pre-eclampsia. A fatal blood clot. An emergency c-section you just don't wake up from.

So many different ways to die while creating life. So many things to fear.

Most women, of course, don't think about any of this: or, if they do, it's with that blythe knowledge that these are things that always happen to someone else.

They're not, though.

The miscarriage and the ectopic pregnancy, for example, both happened to my mum, who had a miscarriage before she had me, and an ectopic pregnancy a few years after I arrived.

I grew up knowing that being pregnant didn't necessarily mean you were going to have a baby. Sometimes it just meant you were going to go through some horrific ordeal, and possibly end up dying in the process. Even just *trying* to have a baby was so fraught with danger, as far as I was concerned, that by far the safest thing to do was to *just not try*.

So I wouldn't. Simple.

But it wasn't *quite* so simple as that, of course. There were just so many reasons not to want children - pregnancy, childbirth, those difficult teenage years - that I proceeded through my teens, twenties, and most of my thirties, absolutely steadfast in my belief that I wouldn't have any: I just didn't want them. I would never be someone's mummy: I would always be Amber - and I was absolutely fine with that.

Then came the second me.

The Second Me

The second me arrived in my late 30s, at roughly the time when all of my friends abruptly, and almost simultaneously, started breeding.

At first I was horrified and confused: even a bit disappointed, if I'm honest. Why had they done it? What were they thinking? Parenthood seemed like such a negative experience to me: all that talk of sleepless nights and dirty nappies, and not being able to go to the bathroom unaccompanied for, oooh, five years, at least.

All of these things horrified me, but the last one most of all. If I had a child, I wouldn't even be able to *go to the bathroom* alone? I don't know about you, but most of my bathroom breaks take two minutes, tops. Would a baby *really* not allow me even *two minutes* of privacy? Not even *two minutes* to just be *myself?*

"You'll see," the people who were already parents would chortle mirthlessly. "Babies need to be held constantly, and toddlers won't leave you alone: it's easier just to take them with you..."

This did not sound like an acceptable solution to me, but my friends all dropped like flies. One after another, the pregnancy announcements came, then the babies themselves. And slowly, something started to change.

At first, the change was slight, and almost imperceptible. I liked the babies: they were cute, after all, and I had never really thought that about babies before. I still didn't want one of my own, though: or, at least, I didn't want to *have* one of my own. Pregnancy terrified me; childbirth even more. I'd suffered severe health anxiety for over a decade at that point: I knew I just couldn't risk the horrors that lurked down that nine month long tunnel - the one where the only light at the end came from the operating theatre lights they'd presumably have to cut me open underneath. No thanks.

I could not do it.

I would not do it.

And then I turned 40.

"I think you should try to consider what you really want from life," Terry had told me, the year before that landmark birthday. "I just worry that one day you might look back and regret not trying."

So I thought about it.

I thought about it for over a year. I imagined what it would feel like to hold my own child in my arms: to say to my parents, "Look: meet your grandchild!" I thought about what he or she would be like, this potential person. Would s/he have my red hair, Terry's dark eyes? Would s/he be happy and extroverted, like him, or shy and awkward, like me?

Most of all, I thought about all the stories I would tell them. The stories of my own life so far, and those of my family. I'd tell them about the time their dad had to have a kidney transplant, and their Uncle John stepped up to donate, as if it was nothing at all. I'd tell them about the time I fell off my bike when I was 12: how I cried when I turned 16. I'd tell them that once upon a time, there was a red-haired girl called Agnes, who had smashed up every piece of crockery in the kitchen of the house she worked in, when she was wrongly accused of stealing. I'd tell them that girl was their great-great-grandmother: that she had a baby girl called Anna, who had a baby girl called Norma, who had a baby girl who was me. "And then I had you," I would say - and another chapter would begin.

I thought of all of these things, and thinking them made them real: made them actual possibilities. Then I thought about the other possible world: the one I was in *now*, in which none of this could happen, because I was too afraid to try. The one in which there's no one left to tell the stories to, and they all end with me.

"OK," I said to Terry one day in April, the month after my 40th birthday. "I think we should give it a try, and see what happens."

And then the world changed again.

The Third Me

The third me was born on August 6th, 2016 - the day the pregnancy test I hadn't even expected I'd need to take, gave me two fat blue lines.

That was a sunny day, too - or, at least, the morning was. Terry and I took our coffee (decaf for me: I was taking no risks) out into the garden, and we sat there talking about how the world had changed.

It felt nothing like I'd expected it to: that was that strange thing.

Right up until the moment I saw the two lines on the stick, I wasn't sure I wanted it: wasn't sure I would cope. I felt sure that if the test was positive, I would instantly regret it - I imagined my legs crumpling beneath me: me falling to the floor, like some kind of third-rate Hitchcock heroine, in a pool of green silk. I had no idea why my mind kept giving me a green silk dressing gown in these imaginings, but I bought one anyway, and wore it when I walked shakily downstairs to tell Terry the news.

My hands were trembling as I handed him the test stick, but I did not collapse, and I did not regret it. I didn't ever regret it: not even when I thought about childbirth, or ectopic pregnancy, or the high risk of miscarriage, particularly for women in my age group. I felt - and this is stupid, obviously - that as the decision to even try for a baby had been so incredibly hard, that fate would somehow intervene, and the universe would make sure that the rest of the process was easy. The thing is, though, I've never actually believed in fate. And I was right not to, because there's no such thing.

The universe had no grand plan for me - or, if it did, it was a particularly cruel one. My body was not trying to tell me something when my period returned instantly, after a decade on the mini pill - and snapped right into a super-regular cycle.

There is no such thing as fate.

I changed my entire world for nothing: and now I have to try to change it back.

Because today I am no longer the first me, or the second. I'm definitely not the 3rd: the one I knew for just three weeks, but who I liked most of all.

So who am I now?

* * *

In my bedside drawer, there's a white envelope, and inside the envelope are three photos: screenshots of the little person-that-never-was, from my six week scan last week.

I haven't opened the envelope: I haven't even looked at it. I guess Terry might even have moved it for me - like he did with the 8 positive pregnancy tests and those 'Poorly Pouches' that arrived too late.

I haven't opened the envelope, but I won't throw it away, either, like the diary I threw away on the morning of the scan that confirmed the miscarriage: the one with the dates of all of my upcoming appointments written in red ink.

8 week scan.

Midwife appointment.

12 week scan.

All of them cancelled. I imagine someone logging onto a computer somewhere in the hospital ward, finding my name in the appointments calendar, hitting DELETE. All that hope, gone in a second.

I threw away the diary (realising too late that all of my passwords were written in the back of it: whoops!), but I can't do much about the photos taken during the last three weeks of my life.

Oh God, the photos.

I went through them all today, on my first day back at work since it happened. Yesterday was sunny, so we took the day off, went out for afternoon tea: a sad parody of the fun days out we had before it happened. Today, though, I had to work: because when you're self-employed, there's no one to step in and do it for you, miscarriage or not.

Work for me consists of writing about my life on the internet. Yeah, I know it's weird, you don't have to tell me. It's a strange way to make a living, for sure, but for me it's also a very natural one, given the passion I've always had for documenting my life. It's why I started blogging in the first place: and why I decided to have a baby, come to think of it: because it suddenly occurred to me to wonder who I was documenting it all *for*. Who would one day read the stories I wrote, and feel something more than just the passing interest of a curious stranger?

Who, indeed.

When I got pregnant, it felt even more important to document it. It was the biggest, most important thing that had ever happened to me, after all, and while it was still too early to write about it on my blog, I could at least take photos: photos my readers would think were just shots of my outfits and days out, but which I'd one day look back on with my future child and say, "Look! This was the day after I found out I was expecting you!" or "This was the day we saw you on the ultrasound for the first time!"

Those three short weeks of pregnancy were sunny and warm, so there are plenty of photos to remember them by. Too many, in fact. I wanted to do my best to make everything feel as normal as possible - mostly just to convince myself that this hadn't been a huge mistake, and that I'd still be able to be *me*, and to go about my life as usual, even though this huge change was taking place inside me. So we had days out, we went to lunch - and everywhere we went, we took the camera and snapped away, making memories to last a lifetime.

Now, of course, there will be no one to look back on those memories but me and Terry: and the memories they hold are almost too painful to bear. Look! This was the day the miscarriage started! I didn't know it yet, but that little circle I'd seen on the ultrasound, just a few days before, had already started to slip away, and by the time I came to look back at those photos, I'd be a different person altogether.

And look! This was the day after my parents found out! They couldn't stop smiling and talking about how excited they were... and, exactly one week later, it was all over.

Unhappy memories: memories I had no choice but to look back at today, as I prepared to post the photos on my blog, accompanied with text which makes absolutely no mention of the *real* story behind those happy, sunlit shots. Well, it was either that or switch the blog to radio silence until I feel better - and what if I never do? I may be a different person now, but I still have to eat, and to pay the mortgage: the show must go on, and so today I sat down and as I scrolled through those photos, I found myself looking at my own happy, hopeful face, and feeling sorry for myself in this odd, almost impersonal way.

"Poor woman," I thought, looking at a photo of myself smiling on a sunny day, just three days before my world came crashing down around me. "What a shame that such a horrible thing happened to her."

Me. It happened to *me*. And two months later, it happened again.

The Expected Ectopic

This time, the pregnancy was ectopic.

I'd always known it would be, of course. When I booked an early scan with my first pregnancy - the one that ended in miscarriage - I remember the sonographer asking why I was there: why did I feel the need for a 6 week scan, when it was unlikely she'd be able to see anything of note?

"I want a scan because I'm convinced it'll be ectopic," I told her, lying down on the bed, and preparing for the worst. And I *was* convinced: so much so, in fact, that as soon as the second line appeared on the test stick, I'd packed a hospital bag, in preparation for the inevitable hospital trip I felt certain was in my future.

I was right, too: I just got the timing slightly wrong. It wasn't *that* pregnancy that was to turn out to be ectopic - it was the *next* one.

When I turned up at the early pregnancy unit, just two months after my miscarriage, I was, once again, asked why I was there. Why did I want a blood test to confirm my pregnancy? Why was I asking for a scan?

"Because I've had three very faint positive tests, and three negative ones," I said, struggling to hold back the tears. "And I'm absolutely sure it means it's ectopic."

And, of course, it was.

Later, once everything was over, and I was back at the EPU, finally being discharged after four week's worth of methotrexate treatment to end a pregnancy that could have killed me if it had continued, the nurse told me how shocked she'd been when my worst fears had been confirmed.

"It just seemed so unlikely that the person who was so convinced she'd have an ectopic pregnancy would be the one to end up actually having one," she told me. It had never seemed unlikely to me, though. I had always been quietly convinced that if I ever got pregnant, I'd end up having either a miscarriage, an ectopic, or both.

I had both.

As it turns out, what doesn't kill you doesn't always make you stronger: sometimes, in fact, it almost completely destroys you instead. And, because of that, I now knew one thing for sure: I would not make the same mistake again.

Week 4
A New Chapter

May 3rd, 2017

I made the same mistake again. Because OF COURSE I did.

Why?

Because there are certain events in everyone's lives that have the ability to split everything into 'Before' and 'After'- and nothing that occurs in The After can ever be the same as it was in The Before.

I remember when my gran died, I scribbled out the date on the calendar that hung in my room – almost scoring through the paper with a big, black X. I was trying to obliterate it – as if crossing the date off the calendar would somehow cross it out of existence, and make it not have happened – but all I succeeded in doing was drawing attention to it: emphasising it, so that every time I was in that room, my eyes were constantly drawn to that big black X on the wall. When I think about my childhood now, everything comes either Before or After that date, which I have never forgotten, even although it was almost 30 years ago now. It was The First Before – but it wasn't, of course, the last, because the fact is that life contains many of these dividing days, lurking innocently in the calendar for years and years, until one day they're singled out for a big black X of their own. Not everything that comes After is bad, obviously – life doesn't work that way – but it IS all After, and wow, but it's an adjustment.

My ectopic pregnancy was one of those events: but so was the death of our precious dog, Rubin, just two and a half months later. When Rubin died, everything suddenly seemed to be After. I felt like all of the good things in my life were now gone, and that all that was left was a slow circling towards old age and inevitable heartache.

(One of the things you're going to learn about me if you continue reading this diary is that 'Drama' is my middle name. Don't say I didn't warn you.)

(It's not: it's Louise. 'Drama' would have been more appropriate, though.)

Of course, one of the hardest things (but also one of the most comforting, I think) to come to terms with in all of this is the fact that you never really know you're living in the Before until you aren't any more. And while that terrible time of my life felt like the beginning of an apparently endless After, I was plagued with the feeling that it could just be the start of another Before.

And so we decided to try again.

Trust me: nobody was more surprised by that decision than I was.

I have never been a risk-taker. I don't ride the roller-coasters that scare me. I don't break the speed limit, or cross the street when the sign tells me not to. I am scared of almost everything, but the thing that scares me most is the thought of hospitalisation, medical procedures and – worst of all – general anaesthetic. These things absolutely terrify me – in a way that I can't even hope to make you understand, because, even at the absolute height of my terror, even *I* know I'm being completely and utterly irrational.

I was absolutely terrified of getting pregnant again: terrified I'd have another miscarriage, scared beyond belief that I might have another ectopic.

Despite that, we decided to try again: decided that, if we were going to have regrets, we'd rather regret trying, than regret giving up.

I *did* regret trying, though: almost immediately, in fact.

Because the evidence was incontrovertible, really: my body was not good at being pregnant. It didn't even know where to put the damn thing, for God's sake. It had gotten things catastrophically wrong two times already, and there was absolutely nothing to suggest that this third attempt would be any more successful: which is why I knew beyond a shadow of a doubt that I *would* get pregnant. All of the things I feared would definitely come to pass (Oh yeah: the other thing you should know about me is that I'm just a little bit of a fatalist), which is why, the night before my period was due, I prepared to meet my fate in a, 'The Condemned Woman Ate a Hearty Meal,' kind of way, only without the 'hearty meal' bit, because I felt too sick with nerves to actually eat.

Instead, I cleaned the house from top to bottom. (Well, from top to top, rather: we're in the middle of a kitchen renovation right now, so the top floor is the only one that's actually livable.) I frantically tried to get ahead with work, knowing I probably wouldn't feel like blogging once the whole 'Will it be a miscarriage or will it be an ectopic?' drama kicked in the next morning. I double-checked the hospital bag, which was still packed from the ectopic: I'd been lucky enough to escape surgery that time, but who knew what kind of horrors awaited me this time around?

Then, with all of that done, I went to bed and lay awake most of the night, my stomach lurching with fear at the thought of the pregnancy test I'd laid out in the bathroom, waiting to be used the next day.

I knew. I just *knew*. Not in a hippy, new-age kind of way, I hasten to add: just in an annoyingly pessimistic, why-can't-I-be-normal kind of way. I was terrified of being pregnant, so being pregnant was obviously what I would be.

And I was.

Unlike the ectopic, this time the second line appeared on the test stick before I'd even finished using it. Unlike the first time this happened, I didn't freak out with nervous excitement: I just calmly walked out of the bathroom and handed the positive test to Terry - remembering too late that I'd just peed on it. Whoops. SORRY Terry.

After that, we got dressed, and drove down the hill to break the news to my parents.

With my first two pregnancies, we'd wanted to keep the secret for as long as possible: I'd had all kinds of cute announcement ideas, and I couldn't wait to use them.

This time, though, there didn't seem to be much point in hiding what I was sure was destined to be yet another tragedy: I knew I'd need as much support as I could get if/when the inevitable happened, so we figured we might as well tell them right away, so they could brace themselves for another few weeks of drama.

"We've got something to tell you," I announced as we walked through the door. "Is it about the dishwasher?" asked my mum, coming out of the kitchen with a panicked look on her face. It took me a good few seconds to remember that, up until this morning, our brand new, but very leaky, dishwasher, had been the biggest issue facing us that week. Oh to be able to worry about the dishwasher again!

It wasn't about the dishwasher, though.

Instead, it was this weird and possibly wonderful piece of news: this thing that would, under any other circumstances, have filled my parents with joy, but which now simply made us all wonder how on earth we were supposed to feel *this* time.

It wasn't like it is in the movies: which was disappointing, really, because, even when you're old enough to know better, you always secretly want things to be just like the movies, don't you? Or even a really cheesy soap opera, say. I mean, is it really too much to hope for just one appropriately cinematic moment? A pregnancy announcement where everyone is happy, and no one starts talking about dishwashers, say? A conversation where someone is ostentatiously listening at the door? Hell, I'd even settle for a classic good twin/ evil twin plot at this point: anything other than this anticlimactic Wednesday morning which could be the start of something wonderful, but ... well, which probably isn't, let's be honest.

And only time will tell.

DAY TWO

Well. I mean. Time will tell... or, obviously, blood tests will tell. The thing is, once you've had one ectopic pregnancy, you have a higher risk of having another one: which is why, after mine, I was told that if I changed my mind (NO), and if I did become pregnant again (NO), I should call the Early Pregnancy Unit right away, so we could begin the whole, terrifying process of blood tests, and waiting for results, and then crying on the bedroom floor when the results came through and weren't what we were hoping for.

Sounds like a fun plan, doesn't it? (NO.)

Nevertheless, it was the only plan we had, so, yesterday morning, just after I'd taken that positive test, Terry called the Early Pregnancy Unit, and asked them if I should come in. I fully expected them to sound the 'Possible Ectopic' klaxon and, I don't know, maybe send an ambulance or something for me, but, actually, they told me it was totally up to me whether I wanted to do the early blood tests or not.

The problem here is that, even if the blood tests *do* indicate that the pregnancy is likely to be ectopic, they won't be able to do anything about it until it can be confirmed on an ultrasound scan... which they won't do until I'm six weeks pregnant.

Thanks to my early testing, of course, I'm currently only *four* weeks pregnant: which means that, if the blood tests suggest it's ectopic, I'll basically just have to live with that knowledge for another fortnight: knowing that the worst is about to happen, but not being able to do a thing about it, other than sit around hoping the tube doesn't rupture this time.

I mean… it doesn't sound like fun, does it?

I'd always assumed that if I ever did get pregnant again, I'd just head straight to the hospital. I would not pass GO. I would most definitely not collect $200.

Knowing that the results won't actually help me at this stage, though, I figure that it's better to travel hopefully than to arrive: so, I've declined the blood tests… for now… on the basis that if I start spotting, say, or have any other reason to believe something might be wrong, I'll go straight in.

We are travelling hopefully. Or, we're trying to, at least.

DAY THREE

The spotting started this morning. Because OF COURSE it did. Off to the hospital. BRB.

DAY FOUR

The waiting room of the Early Pregnancy Unit is exactly as I remember it: right down to the TV in the corner, playing endless episodes of *Homes Under the Hammer,* while a series of white-faced women and their anxious-looking partners sit silently beneath it, waiting for news that will surely change their lives.

Yesterday, of course, I knew *my* news wouldn't be the life-changing variety: or not yet, anyway. It takes at least two blood tests, you see, to work out whether or not a pregnancy is viable: the first one simply confirms that you're pregnant, and gives you a hormone level (HCG, the pregnancy hormone) to use as a starting point, while the next one, taken around 48 hours later, tells you whether that level has risen, fallen, or remained the same.

In a normal, healthy pregnancy, HCG should roughly double every 48 hours.

With my ectopic, the levels started off perilously low, and rose only very slightly: just enough to tell us that there was something very, very wrong. It took two blood tests to get to that point, though, so when lovely Jill, the nurse who'd seen me through both the miscarriage and the ectopic, showed me into her office this morning and smiled sympathetically, the very first thing she did was remind me that the results of today's test were almost irrelevant: that this would not be the *life-changing* news, but simply the common-or-garden variety bad news. .

"Whatever this result is," Jill said, as I held out my arm for the needle, "Try not to read too much into it. Low HCG doesn't necessarily mean the pregnancy is ectopic, or that it isn't viable, so just try to remember that."

With my ectopic, however, that's exactly what the low HCG I'd had on the first test had meant: so as we drove home to our building-site of a house, knowing that we'd have to wait until the next morning for the phone call with the results, we were both feeling pretty nervous.

Actually, though, Jill called at 6pm that night, having stayed late just to get my results back.

"I have some very good news for you," were her opening words. "
You know how I told you not to read too much into this result? Well, scratch that..."

Twenty. Four. Thousand.

My HCG was TWENTY FOUR FREAKING THOUSAND.

Compared to just 180 with the ectopic. So... quite a big difference, then.

"There's no guarantee, of course," Jill said, carefully, "But with this result, we think it's highly unlikely to be another ectopic – we're not concerned at all."

Not concerned.

Highly unlikely.

Twenty. Four. Freaking. THOUSAND.

There's a chance - probably not a good one, if my luck so far is anything to go by, but still, a chance - that I could be having a baby.

Third time lucky?

DAY FIVE

Molar pregnancy.

That's what causes very high HCG.

I know, because I Googled. And yes, OK, 'Thou Shalt Not Google' is the very first of the Health Anxiety Commandments, but, the thing is, once Jill got off the phone, and I'd had time for the news to sink in, I got to thinking. That's always dangerous for me, and this time was no exception, because what I thought was that my HCG levels weren't just high: they were *super* high. *Crazy* high. And what could possibly make them that high, I wondered?

"Twins," said my mum cheerfully, when I called my parents to tell them the good news. "Maybe it's twins!"

So I Googled. And yes, it turns out that twins *can* cause HCG to be high... but so can a molar pregnancy: which, for those of you who haven't spent your adult lives worrying about every single terrible pregnancy-related tragedy that can befall you, is one of the few things in the world that I would class as Even Worse Than an Ectopic.

A molar pregnancy happens when an egg is fertilized, but, instead of developing into a normal fetus, grows into an abnormal cluster of cells. Molar pregnancies can take a long time to resolve, and sometimes require chemotherapy, or my old friend, methotrexate, to deal with them. Molar pregnancies are my new worst nightmare: so, naturally, I'm completely convinced that a molar pregnancy is exactly what I have. "My body's just going to cycle through every single terrible pregnancy-related outcome it can think of," I told Terry tearfully last night. "I mean, I've had the miscarriage, I've had the ectopic – *of course* I'd have to have a molar next!"

Even Terry didn't have the words to reassure me on this one: *that's* how badly the previous two losses have affected us - they've turned my usually optimistic husband into someone who, like me, has come to always expect the worst. Which is quite possibly the saddest thing about this horrible situation.

The most *frustrating* thing about it, meanwhile, is the fact that I won't have my next blood test until tomorrow, and probably won't have the results until the day after. Meanwhile, the spotting continues: Lovely Jill tells me not to worry - that spotting is relatively common in early pregnancy, and that it doesn't necessarily mean something is wrong. Of course, Lovely Jill said that the last time, and the time before that, so while it's not getting any worse, and I'm assuming that has to be a good sign, this whole situation now has a depressing air of familiarity about it.

I am no longer travelling quite so hopefully.

Week 5
The Tell-Tale Heart

It's not a molar. And it's not an ectopic, either.

It's a *baby*, people. A real, live baby.

We found out on a Friday, after another sleepless night, and another early start, after which we basically just sat around waiting for Jill to start work, so we could finally find out the results of the second blood test.

"As soon as I put the phone down after our last conversation," she said, when Terry called her on the dot of nine, "I kicked myself, because I knew Amber would Google it, and assume the high HCG meant it was a molar. It doesn't, though, you can relax."

With an ectopic pregnancy, HCG rises slowly. With a molar, it rises very, very fast.

Mine, on the other hand?

My HCG had risen by exactly the amount you'd expect it to in a normal, healthy pregnancy.

Which was honestly the *last* thing I expected to hear. I mean, "normal" and "healthy" in relation to a pregnancy of mine? This was uncharted territory: soon, however, we were to be back on familiar ground, apparently, because the other piece of news Jill had to impart to us was that the HCG levels were now high enough that we'd have a good chance of being able to see something on an ultrasound.
"We don't feel it's really necessary at this stage," Jill told us, "Because the blood results so far are indicating everything's fine. If it would help to put your mind at rest, though, we're happy to book you in for this afternoon, if you'd like?"

Yes. We would like. We would very much like.

And also, of course, we would very much NOT like. Because, as we drove back to the hospital early that afternoon, I couldn't help but think of the *other* ultrasounds: the ones that *hadn't* given me the results I was hoping for.

This, after all, would be my fifth scan: which, for a woman with no children, seemed a little bit much, really. All but the very first scan had ended with the words, "I'm sorry, but..." It was impossible to believe that this one would be any different, so, as I walked into the same booth, in the same room my miscarriage had been confirmed in, and lay down on the same narrow bed, staring at the same dark patch on the ceiling, I was already shaking so much I wasn't sure they'd even be able to go ahead.

The sonographer's name was Julie. She was so kind that I wanted to ask if I could take her home with me. "Of course, you're scared," she said, as she squirted clear gel on my stomach (Everyone always describes the gel as cold. It's actually quite warm, though: fun fact for you, there...), "You've only ever had bad news from scans in the past, but let's see if we can set your mind at rest with this one..."

And she did. It took a regular scan *and* an internal one to do it, but finally Julie straightened up and turned the screen towards us.

"I'VE FOUND IT!" she said, sounding so genuinely excited that it makes me cry to remember it. "It's in the right place! And you know what? It's really, really small, but I *think* I can even see a heartbeat..."

That was yesterday.
At some point in the last week or so, a tiny little heart started beating: a tiny little heart that, all being well, will continue to beat long after I'm gone, and all of the stress of this pregnancy long forgotten. The tiny little heart will be the start of a new chapter: a new Before AND a new After.

The tiny little heart is *everything*, basically. And all I have to do now is keep it alive for the next eight months. No biggie, then...

Week 6
Boobwatch 2017

And, after all of that - all of the stress and the excitement and the fear - everything went back to normal.

No, I mean that literally: as in, I feel totally normal. Normal in a "Cannot Possibly Be Pregnant" kind of way. Even the spotting stopped just a few hours after the ultrasound, almost as if it knew the jig was up, and it was time to stop messing with me: and while the anxiety didn't stop with it (Apologies for the TMI, but I'm basically on permanent knicker watch right now, with each trip to the bathroom requiring superhuman levels of courage from me...), physically, at least, I'm feeling absolutely *fine*. Which is a worry, isn't it?

Where is the crippling nausea, the bizarre food aversions, the frequent need to pee? Where is the weird metallic taste in the mouth that I had with the ectopic, or the increased sensitivity to smell that my mum always talks about having when she was expecting me? ("I could actually smell dirt," she always says, looking oddly pleased about this. "*DIRT*.")

And, I mean, it's not like I want to be able to smell dirt (DIRT) obviously. Well, OK, maybe just a *little* bit of dirt, say. Just enough to reassure me that I am actually pregnant, and I haven't just imagined it, because right now I'm not so sure. In fact, if it wasn't for that grainy little black and white photo, which Lovely Julie printed out for us at the scan, and which, to be totally honest, doesn't look like anything more than a blob to me, I would definitely be starting to wonder.

Well, that and my boobs, obviously. It would be hard to forget my boobs right now: mostly because I actually *have* some, for the first time in my life, but also because, wow, they *hurt*. And then they don't. And then they do! And then not. And this cycle goes on and on, to the point I'm at now, where the only thing I do all day is sit and repeatedly prod my own boobs, just to see if they're still sore (PREGNANT!) or not. (NOT.) Honestly, it's fortunate that I don't have a "real" (By which I mean "traditional") job, because I can't even imagine how women who work in offices, say, or, who have public-facing roles, manage to get away with the constant boob prodding. Or is that just me?

Regardless of how normal or otherwise this is (And, I mean, I think we all know it's "otherwise", don't we?) there's no getting away from the fact that Boobwatch 2017 is ON. I've prodded my boobs at least 7 times while I was writing this diary entry, for instance. I think they're maybe a *little* bit tender, but that *could* just be from all the prodding, obviously, so, BRB, just going to prod them again to be sure...

How I feel about this pregnancy right now totally depends on the status of the Boobwatch. If the boobs are sore, I feel momentarily reassured... until a few minutes later, when I start to think I might have just imagined the soreness, so I check again, and, is it just me, or did they not feel *quite* so tender that time?

I know that this is crazy, obviously. I know symptoms come and go, and that if my boobs stop hurting, it doesn't necessarily mean I'm about to miscarry. With my first pregnancy, though, that's exactly what it *did* mean, so it doesn't really matter how often the collective wisdom of *Mumsnet* tells me that I shouldn't read too much into the disappearing symptoms: I'm going to worry anyway - and I'm going to keep on prodding my boobs.

On the plus side, though, I haven't wanted to drink coffee since the day I found out I was pregnant, even though I normally can't even get out of bed without a huge mug of the stuff. That has to be a good sign, right?

I just wish I could smell dirt, though.

Is it too much to ask for just a *little* bit of dirt?

Week 7
Be Careful What You Wish For

Last night as we were watching TV, I realised I could smell Terry's breath: and also the blanket that's been draped over the back of the sofa for as long as I can remember, without me ever once realising it had a smell. (Or, indeed, realising it needed a wash, obviously. Must get on that: just as soon as I can persuade myself to get off this sofa, that is...)

I was absolutely delighted. Not about the blanket, of course: because that thing is gross, and the knowledge that it's been secretly smelling like that all this time, but I've only just realised it, has awakened a deep sense of shame, which I will have to add to my list of 'Things I Will Think About When I'm Not Feeling Sick,' because here's the other big news from last night:

I started feeling sick. Like, really, really sick. And, honestly, it wasn't as awesome as I'd thought it would be, really. Reassuring, yes. I wanted to feel sick because at least it would be a definite pregnancy symptom, and I could finally stop prodding my stupid boobs all the damn time, but, as it turns out... well, let's just say that we were watching 'Anne With an E' on Netflix at the time, and I will never look at that spunky little redhead in quite the same way again, because this is definitely one of those things to file under 'Be Careful What You Wish For.'

It's a mistake, for instance, to wish for morning sickness - or late evening sickness, as the case may be. Because feeling sick is not fun, is it? And neither is being able to smell your husband's breath, come to think of it. So, I spent my evening clutching the plastic bowl which I ran right out and bought the first time I found out I was pregnant, and praying that I wouldn't actually have to use it.

I didn't, thankfully. But I suspect my time is coming, and while part of me still feels nothing but relief about that, another part of me has just this second remembered that she is borderline phobic about vomit. So that'll be fun, no?

Speaking of Terry, meanwhile, it's not just his breath that's annoying: he's also determined to make sure my pregnancy diet is as nutritious as possible, which means he's spent the entire week trying to make me eat fish.

I hate fish.

On second thoughts, maybe that's the reason I've been feeling so sick?

Week 8
Morning, Noon and Night Sickness

Things That Have Made Me Cry This Week:

1. Terry brought me watermelon and picked out all of the seeds. (Good tears)

2. The story on the news of the zookeeper killed by a tiger. (Bad tears)

3. Terry brought me toast cut into "soldiers" and I thought about how my dad used to make me a boiled egg with toast soldiers when I was a little girl. (No idea)

4. Writing the above sentence about the toast soldiers.

5. Terry tried to make me eat a croissant. I did not want to eat a croissant.

6. Throwing up. Throwing up makes me cry. I've done a LOT of crying this week, needless to say.

Back in my childfree days, people would often ask me why I didn't want to have children, and I would give them a variety of different answers, ranging from, "I just *don't*, OK?" to, "I dunno, why don't *you* want to mind your own business?" depending on how sassy I was feeling at the time.

The real reason, though - or one of them, at least - was that I didn't want to have to deal with morning sickness.

It's been easy to forget this over the past few weeks, when I've been so desperate for confirmation that I was actually pregnant that I was even praying for nausea, but I really, really don't like vomiting. And, I mean, who does, right? Show me the person who claims to enjoy throwing up, and I will show you a liar or a masochist. No one wants to be sick all the time: I, however, am so scared of throwing up that, up until this year, I couldn't even fathom why anyone would want to risk getting pregnant when it was practically guaranteed to make you sick. I'm still wondering, to be totally honest.

My body hates me. I'm convinced it secretly wants me to die – and when I was crouched next to the toilet on Monday afternoon, feeling like I would *literally* never stop throwing up, and that this would just be my life from now on, I almost wanted it to succeed in that mission. I was totally ready to hold up the white flag and say, "Sweet release of death, come take me now!" But I didn't. And I'm getting ahead of myself here.

So, week 8 started suspiciously smoothly. Each new week begins on a Saturday for me, and this Saturday was a fairly uneventful one: in fact, I was feeling well enough to get dressed, run a comb through my hair (no makeup other than lipstick, though – that would've been WAY too ambitious...) and go out with Terry to our favourite cafe for some cake. (Which would normally have been coffee and cake, but coffee is the very LAST thing I want right now, so, in my case, it was cake and a carton of Capri Sun, which I promptly spilled all over the table. Hey, imagine me being in charge of a whole new life in just a few months time! Gulp.)

Anyway, having spent the past few days in PJs or sweat pants, with no makeup, and my hair scraped back in a scraggy pony tail (Which, by the way, does NOT look simple and elegant on me, like it does on other people. Why can't I be a beautiful, fragile looking pregnant person? Why do I have to look like I just finished a three-day bender all the time?), this was a small victory, and I even indulged in some gentle, "Why do I have no symptoms today? There must be something wrong!" reasoning – much to the frustration of the long-suffering Terry, who says that it's totally normal for symptoms to come and go, but whose eyes light up with relief every time I tell him I feel nauseous. Or maybe he just secretly hates me?

The next day, however, was a different matter altogether. This was the day I didn't get out of bed until 9pm, in fact, having felt so nauseous that I ended up throwing up in the bathroom, and then lying in bed for the rest of the day, desperately hoping it wouldn't happen again. And, I mean, I thought *that* was pretty bad – like, *the worst*, really. Then Monday arrived, and on Monday I threw up until my throat ached and there was nothing left to throw up, but my stupid body decided to keep on trying anyway: thanks, body! Hate you too!

By the time it was over, I was in tears, and telling Terry that I just couldn't do this – absolutely not. In my mind, I kept hearing my mum cheerfully tell me about how she'd had "morning" sickness for the full 9 months when she was pregnant with me, and was still throwing up when she arrived at the hospital for the birth. I knew beyond doubt that I would NOT cope with that – that I would LITERALLY DIE – so I was a sorry, sorry state that day, lying in bed eating ice lollies in a bid to get some fluids without having to drink them: for some reason, I can eat, but I can't drink: I'm constantly thirsty, but the thought of all of that liquid sloshing around inside me makes me feel like... sorry, BRB, have to barf...

Where was I?

Oh yeah: that day I was sicker than I think I've ever been in my life. Nevertheless, I managed to get out of bed by 4pm, which was at least better than the day before. Terry described this as "a better day". I described it as, "one of the worst days of my life so far" – an observation compounded by the fact that, as soon as I tried to go to sleep that night, I started feeling sick again: GAH.

Tuesday, however, actually was a better day. On Tuesday, we decided to try to tackle the nausea head on, by taking the advice everyone gives you to try to keep eating small amounts throughout the day, so your stomach is never totally empty. (Yeah, yeah, I know I should have taken this advice sooner, but you try choking down a ginger biscuit when a) You feel like you're about to throw up, and, b) You freakin' hate ginger biscuits, and then get back to me, OK?) So I started the day with a slice of dry toast, which was every bit as unappetising as it sounds, and then continued with regular doses of fruit (mostly for fluid), salt and vinegar crisps, plus the dreaded ginger biscuits, which I honestly have no idea why I'm persisting with, because, YUCK.

Anyway, I've no idea whether this technique actually worked, or whether it was just coincidence, but I didn't throw up that day, and I even felt well enough to wash my hair, get dressed (makeup still far beyond my capabilities: saving a fortune on products, here!), and head down to the local library to stock up on reading material. As is usual with me, reading is the only thing that's been helping me stay vaguely calm, and it was getting quite expensive to keep on buying new books for my Kindle, so it's back to the library I go, just like in the olden days. I'd say it was working out well for me, but I seem to have developed an uncanny knack of only picking books in which someone either has a miscarriage or dies in childbirth, so, yeah, *not really*.

The rest of the week followed a similar kind of pattern, with the nausea and the toast and the wanting to die, but now there was a plot twist in the form of a crippling headache, the likes of which I've never seen before. So, I basically have a really bad hangover all the time, in other words, only without the fun drinking part before it. (Also without the feeling of doom after it, in which I lie in bed worrying about all of the stupid things I probably said while I was drunk, though. So at least that's something.)

On Friday morning, however, there came the merest sliver of a silver lining when I had my first meeting with the midwife who'll (hopefully) be looking after me for the duration of the pregnancy.

Now, I was actually pretty nervous about this meeting, because what if the midwife turned out to be one of those old-school hospital matron types, who'd just be all, ''Don't be silly dear, baby comes first!'' when I tried to tell her all of the things I'm worried about: and, the thing is, there are a *lot* of things I'm worried about right now.

Things I Am Worried About

1. Hospitals.
2. Communal wards in hospitals.
3. Being left on my own on a communal ward in hospital, while I'm either in the early stages of labour, or waiting to be induced, just like my friend Lindsay, whose husband was sent home as soon as the pessary went in.
4. Having to be induced.
5. Being left alone in the hospital right after the baby is born, because there are no husbands allowed on the communal ward, so I just have to look after a whole new person by myself, even though I haven't the slightest idea how to do that.
6. Dying in childbirth.
7. The baby dying in childbirth.
8. No one dies, but I sustain some terrible injury which ruins the rest of my life.
9. Having to have a general anaesthetic.

And that's just off the top of my head, too. The more I start to think about the various items on the list, the longer the list gets, until I find myself lying awake at night worrying about how I'll cope if the person in the bed next to me decides to listen to music through those crappy little headphones everyone has, so I just have to lie awake all night after the birth, listening to the relentless thump of someone else's bass. I didn't bring that one up at the meeting, though. No, I'm just going to save that for the next one, I think. Also, at this first meeting, I found myself torn between the desire to appear "normal" (Always a challenge, obviously, but I've noticed that people seem to like "normal" people more than they like... well, ME, basically... so I do my best.), and pretend everything is fine, or to admit that I'm totally batshit, but at least get some kind of reassurance on all of this.

In the end, I went with ''Totally Batshit', and, luckily for me, the midwife - Lovely Carolyn - was kind enough to pretend not to notice. She was also, thankfully, kind enough to listen to what I had to say, and assure me she'd do her absolute best to get me through the next 8 months with at least some of my sanity intact.

She did confirm two of my biggest fears: that partners are not allowed to stay on the ward overnight, and that it's not possible to book a private room, even if you pay for it. This was a huge blow, obviously, because while I know everyone will assume I'm just being an absolute princess by wanting my own room, and for my husband to stay with me, the truth is, hospitals terrify me. I think it's the smell of them. And the fact that there are always people dying in them, obviously. And the complete lack of privacy in them, when you're expected to sit around in your nightie, in a room full of other people and their visitors, at a time when you're at your most vulnerable and scared. There are just so many reasons to fear hospitals, really, and I don't want to be left on my own in a place that terrifies me. I just can't do it.

I don't, however, want to have a home birth either, which I guess would be the most logical solution for someone with a fear of hospitals. My fear of dying in childbirth is even greater than my fear of hospitals, though, and it turns out that just keeping the baby inside me forever isn't an option either, so the hospital it is.

The answer to the biggest question of all, though - how the hell am I going to get this baby out of me? - was surprisingly simple. We'll get the baby out, said Caroline, by doing whatever we have to do to make the process as easy, and as non-traumatic as possible. Given that my birth plan so far could be summed up by the line, "I want us to both be alive at the end of it," that works just fine for me.

And the good news, of course, is that, however I decide to give birth, I at least have a lot of time to work it out. Or, at least, I hope so, anyway.

Week 9
The Sadness of
the Ham Sandwich

Yesterday I had my third ultrasound: this one was mostly
needed to date the pregnancy, so I can book the Harmony
blood test for next week (It can only be done after 10 weeks),
but, for me, it was mostly about reassurance. Over the past few
days I'd once again managed to convince myself that
something had gone wrong (For no reason other than that "bad
feeling" I always get. Terry keeps trying to point out that if I
always get that feeling, then it can't actually be trusted, but, of
course, that way of thinking is way too logical for me, and no
amount of logic will talk me out of a "feeling"), so I was, as
usual, absolutely terrified going into this appointment – even
more so this time, because this was the first ultrasound I'd had
since the nausea got bad, and I was really worried about having
to drink a pint of water and then have someone press down on
my stomach: I mean, seriously?

At the hospital, we had a longer wait than usual, during which
I saw quite a few pregnant women go in, and then re-emerge
clutching scan photos. Because I'm me, the more of this I saw,
the more convinced I became that I wouldn't get to be one of
them: I was almost sick with nerves by the time I lay down on
the couch, but thankfully the sonographer took only a few
seconds to locate the baby, and find the heartbeat – at which
point I obviously burst into tears.

We left with our own set of scan photos, in a little cardboard
wallet with 'HELLO BABY' on the front a little wallet– which I
was still staring at 20 minutes later in the pharmacy waiting
room when two friends of Terry's mum walked in and looked
right at it: so much for secrecy, huh?

At any other time, I think I'd have been quite worried about this in case one of them bumped into her, and spilled the beans, but, as it happened, we'd already decided that, if everything was OK, we'd go straight to Terry's mum's house from the hospital and tell her. She's been quite unwell lately, and is waiting on some medical results of her own right now, so we thought it might be good for her to have some happy news to focus on for a while. I was really glad we told her, too – we obviously had to try to temper her excitement a little and explain that it's still very early, but she was absolutely thrilled, and had a bit of a cry (a good one, obviously!) when we told her, so it was nice to see her so happy and excited after everything she's been through. Now we just have to hope that everything continues to go well…

On that note, we were at the pharmacy because when I went to see the nurse at the Early Pregnancy Unit after my scan (They always want us to just check in with them afterwards), I mentioned the nausea, and she went and got me a prescription for Cyclizine, which I can take if it gets really bad. I filled the prescription, but I have no intention of taking the pills, because even though I know beyond doubt that the doctor wouldn't have prescribed them if there was even the slightest chance of them harming my baby, I just can't stop worrying about it. Things can only get better, after all: right?

So, I kept the pills safely tucked away in my bedside drawer, and, by cunningly refusing to take them, I was able to end Week 9 of this pregnancy by running gagging down the hall (vaguely worried that I *might* be about to throw up on my precious new floor, but also not really caring if I did…), and making it to the downstairs loo just in time to throw up extravagantly in the toilet: so, yeah, I'd say that, on balance, things did NOT, in fact, "get better", although I *wish*.

Other Things That Made Me Cry this Week:

1. A ham sandwich. I couldn't eat it. I could barely even look it. But it was such a beautiful ham sandwich, and Terry had spent time making it, and oh my God, the sadness of the ham sandwich...

2. The fried rice Terry made a late-night dash to the local Chinese takeaway for, when it transpired that I definitely wasn't going to be able to eat the ham sandwich.

3. The Facebook support group for women who are pregnant after an ectopic. So many sad stories. So many dashed hopes. So many tears.

Week 10
Testing Times

Some things I don't believe in:

- God
- Fairies
- Ghosts
- Psychics
- Astrology
- That the earth is flat/ the moon landings were faked / vaccines cause autism
- That "everything happens for a reason"
- That "what's for you won't go past you"
- That wrap dresses are universally flattering

One thing I do quite firmly believe in, even although I know it's stupid, and goes totally against my normal belief system :

That the universe almost certainly has it in for me, and that it will not allow me to experience anything Very Good without also handing me a giant dose of the Very Bad to counteract it.

Case in point: just two weeks after Terry and I got engaged, Terry was diagnosed with end-stage kidney failure, and told that, unless he started dialysis immediately - oh, and had a transplant at some point - he'd die.

It was a bit of a bummer, all things considered, and, quite apart from anything else, it served to confirm my long-held belief that the universe was Out to Get Me. I don't believe in luck. I do, however, believe in *bad* luck, and, for most of my life, I've believed that, if it wasn't for the bad luck, I wouldn't have any luck at all. So, it's kind of a, "The universe gives with one hand, and takes away with the other," kind of deal, basically.

I know it's stupid. I know it makes absolutely no sense. I've felt this for as long as I can remember, though, so I guess it should have come as no surprise that, just a few days after seeing our new baby on the ultrasound scan, we'd find out that Terry's mum has cancer: gastric cancer, to be exact. Which, I mean, thanks, universe. You couldn't let us have just *one* thing, could you?

We found out on Friday, after a long week of waiting. So far, we're hopeful it'll be treatable, but it'll take more tests to establish that for sure, and, in the meantime, we wait. And wait. And waiting has pretty much been the story of this week, really, because while we were waiting on the results of Terry's mum's test, we were also waiting for the results of the Harmony Blood Test, which I had on Sunday morning, with the aim of finding out whether our unborn child is likely to have birth defects which may or may not be compatible with life. No pressure there, then.

So, yeah, I'm really tempted to describe this as a "testing" week, but it's not really the time for bad puns, is it? No. It is not.

I was scared witless, obviously. Not about the test itself: it was just a simple blood test, and, God knows, I've had enough of those over the past few months to have become something of a pro at them. (I WAS, on the other hand, pretty worried that I'd throw up all over the nice private clinic in Edinburgh where we had the test. That's always a possibility for me these days...) No, my fears revolved wholly around the test results: which, we were told, would take around a week, and would tell us with 99% certainty whether or not the baby has Down's Syndrome, or some other kind of life-limiting condition.

I chose to have this test because the alternative was waiting for my 12 week scan, and then allowing the NHS to politely point out that, as a very, very old person (I believe the technical term is "elderly primagravida". Cute, huh?), my child has a higher than average chance of having something seriously wrong with it ... at which point I'd be given the choice between an amniocentesis test (high risk of miscarriage), or spending the rest of the pregnancy worrying myself sick about it. (High risk of going out of my mind.) And neither of those options seemed particularly appealing, you know?

The Harmony Test, on the other hand gives you a much more accurate result, so we headed into Edinburgh early on Sunday morning, and then I got to spend the rest of the week regretting it, and worrying about it - to the point where, by the time the results came in, on Friday morning, I'd basically just given up on life, and spent the entire morning lying on my bed, shaking with anxiety, and then worrying about the shaking and the anxiety, because isn't *that* bad for the baby too? It's been a fun week, for sure.

My test results came back just thirty minutes before Terry's mum's did.

The baby is fine.

Terry's mum is not.

We're hopeful, of course, that Terry's mum *will* be fine in time, and with treatment. But we just don't know that for sure... and, actually, I think I *am* just going to go ahead and make that really bad pun now, all things considered.

It's been a testing week: one of the all-time worsts, in fact. And I'd like to think that things can only get better, but we don't know that either yet. And, once again, all we can do is wait. And in the meantime? We throw up. Or, at least, *I* do, apparently...

Week 11
Impostor Syndrome

Things people tell you will definitely cure morning sickness:

1. Ginger biscuits
2. Dry toast
3. Flat Coke (Er, the fizzy drink, not the white powder...)
4. Eating little and often
5. Peppermint

Things that have definitely not helped with my morning sickness, not even slightly:

1. Ginger biscuits.
2. Dry toast.
3. Flat Coke.
4. Eating little and often.
5. Peppermint.

Seriously, though: if even one more person asks me if I've tried ginger biscuits, I will... well, I'll probably throw up, but that's pretty much the norm right now, anyway. Eating little and often, meanwhile, just means throwing up little and often, and that's not really helpful either, is it?

Nothing is helping. Absolutely nothing. I mean, I spent most of yesterday evening sitting huddled over a plastic basin in my parents garden, absolutely convinced I was about to throw up, and doing everything in my (Admittedly limited) power to prevent it, while simultaneously praying that no one was about to suggest ginger freaking biscuits for the 765th time.

I did this because I'm an asshole, obviously. I mean, I think in this kind of situation, most people would probably rather throw up than endure hours on end of nausea, wouldn't they? I, however, would apparently rather huddle over a basin for hours on a warm summer's night, and so that's exactly what I did.

Honestly, I'd have preferred to have been huddled over the toilet, as that's my preferred vomitin' place, but the sickness struck when I was too far away from it to trust myself not to throw up all the way down the hall, so a plastic basin was produced (Actually, first of all a salad bowl was produced, which was just all kinds of wrong, really: I mean, can you even imagine the family dinners we'd have in the future with *that* sitting on the table in front of us?), and I assumed the "No one touch me, speak to me, or otherwise acknowledge me," position for the next forty minutes or so or hell.

Of course, my parents and Terry kept gamely insisting that it was totes fine if I threw up in the garden, but while I may be a drama queen, I'm not enough of one to want to vomit in front of an audience, so, once the nausea started to recede a little, I got up and made my way to the bathroom, where I spent another 20 minutes battling waves of nausea and wondering why the hell I'd done this to myself.

I wasn't sick. Honestly, by the end of my stint with the basin, though, I was actually starting to wish I would be, just to put an end to it, and that's not like me at. Still, I eventually started feeling a bit better, and returned to the bosom of my family just in time to catch them discussing my pot belly, so that was nice. Ahem.

Anyway, today is Terry's birthday. I got him a baby. (Also a SMEG toaster, but, let's be honest, that bad boy is mostly for ME.) (The baby is also for me, obviously, but I'm going to get years worth of mileage out of this, and you better believe I'll be milking it for all it's worth. Like, "Oh, you bought me that trench coat I wanted for my birthday, this year, Terry? That's nice: I grew you a live human! Inside my body! BEAT THAT, SUCKER." Seriously, if all of my future presents don't have red soles, or come in a little blue box, I will not be happy.)

In other news, I'm getting more and more worried about the 12 week scan. Quelle surprise, non?

The thing is, though, once we got the Harmony results back, and knew that the baby was healthy, Terry insisted on starting to tell the rest of his family the news.

It wasn't how we'd imagined it. This is starting to become a theme.

The first time I was pregnant, we had all kinds of cute - and, OK, totally corny - ideas about how we'd tell our families the news. Terry's mum's illness isn't the only reason we won't be carrying out any of those plans this time around (The miscarriage and the ectopic have played their parts too, by making us both feel much less confident that this pregnancy will result in an actual baby...), but while we know everyone will obviously be happy for us, it just seems a bit crass to expect them to want to celebrate right now, or even just concentrate on something other than the terrible news we got last week.

In the end, then, we went for a very low-key rollout of the news: Terry called one brother, popped in to see another one (Without me: I had a hot date with the sick bowl that day...), and then we told his sister and her family when we met up for his birthday earlier today.

They were, as predicted, all thrilled for us: there were even some comments about how the timing couldn't be better, because lord knows, we all need some good news right now. And, of course, as nice as all of this was, it only served to make me feel like even more of an imposter, really.

I'm just so scared that all of this worry, and all of this hope, is all going to have been for nothing, and that, in a week's time, I'll have my 12 week scan, and all our hopes will come crashing back down. Mostly I feel like we're just constantly lurching from one source of anxiety to the next right now, and it's so, so hard to deal with. I also feel like I can't really consider myself "pregnant" (no matter how hard the morning sickness tries to convince me I am...) until we've had this next scan, so when people start to congratulate us, or talk about the future, I feel like a giant fraud, almost as if I'm lying to them, and don't deserve any of their good wishes. Terry tells me I'm being silly, and that the risk of miscarriage is now very low, but it's hard to shake the worry – roll on Thursday...

Week 12
Good News / Bad News

This week brought very, very good news, and very, very bad news, in equal measures.

The good news is that I had my 12 week scan - that all-important line in the sand that I've been counting down to from the moment I found out I was pregnant - and got to see our perfect, healthy little baby wriggling around, and almost seeming to show off for the camera. That little blob on the screen in the earlier scans has turned into a real, live person - an *actual baby* - and seeing it jumping around in there was as wonderful as it was surreal. Mostly wonderful, though.

The bad news is that Terry's mum's cancer is inoperable.

They've given her six months.

I'm currently three months pregnant.

When I had my miscarriage, people kept on telling me that everything happens for a reason: and, if that's the case, I would really, really like those people to explain to me what possible reason there could be for this particularly clumsy "circle of life" shit the universe seems to be dealing up to us right now.

A birth and a death: is that it? One in, one out? We don't get to just welcome a new life, without having to lose an existing one, first? Or is it just that we're never going to be allowed to fully enjoy any of the good things in life, because they're always going to be overshadowed by the bad?

Needless to say, it's been a tough old week, containing the highest of highs, and the very lowest of lows. I think we've gone through every emotion possible in the space of just a few days, but the one that sticks out the most is this:

It's not fair.

It just isn't.

Soula has taken the news better than any of us. She insists she wants to be here when the baby is born, and I honestly believe she will be: partly because I just can't allow myself to think she won't, but also because she is one of the strongest, most determined people I know, and if anyone can beat this, it would be her.

The thing is, though: she shouldn't really have to, should she? She shouldn't have to "beat" anything: she should just be able to enjoy this time, and look forward to meeting her newest grandchild.

She might not, though.

And it's *just not fair*.

Week 13
The Second Trimester

I'm choosing to deal with the news about Terry's mum by simply refusing to believe it's true. I just *can't* believe it's true. So while I've been doing my best to support her and Terry, and to be there for the rest of the family, I'm going to stick to (mostly) pregnancy-related news here, and, like Scarlett O'Hara, I'll think about The Other Thing tomorrow. Or that's the plan, anyway.

The good news - if there can be said to be "good" news right now - is that Terry's mum herself is doing really well: she doesn't have too many physical symptoms right now, and mentally - well, mentally the woman is a complete inspiration, who's just powering on regardless. I'd always known she was strong (This is a woman who was abandoned on an Athens doorstep as a baby, and whose childhood didn't really get much better from there...), but seriously: the day after her diagnosis, she went to bingo as usual (Us: "Are you sure you want to go to bingo?" Terry's mum: "Well, what else would I be doing on a Tuesday night?"), and the day after *that*, she cooked dinner for 7 people. We did try to dissuade her from this, obviously, and offered to do the cooking for her from now on, but if you've ever met a Greek mother, you'll know you aren't getting out of her house until you've eaten at least your own bodyweight in home-cooked food, and if cancer thinks it's going to stop my mother-in-law from feeding her family, well, cancer doesn't know my mother-in-law, is all I'm saying.

(She did apologise for buying in cakes rather than making them from scratch. She says she'll get to that next week.)

Anyway. Because Terry's mum has been so brave, we've all been basically taking our cue from her, and doing our best to stay calm, even when we feel anything BUT. All of this is obviously much harder than I'm probably making it sound here, though: honestly, it's hard not to feel very 'WHY US?' about it all right now, and I suspect that will be an ongoing battle. For now, though, we're just taking it one day at a time, and trying to appreciate every good day we get: sometimes that's all you can really do, isn't it?

So, as of today, I'm now 13 weeks pregnant. I can't believe I made it to the second trimester: I really wish I could go back in time and tell my post-miscarriage, post-ectopic self that one day I'd be 13 weeks (and still MOSTLY sane, into the bargain...) – I know she wouldn't believe me, but it would maybe have made her a bit less of a miserable sod at the time, huh?

(I would also tell her not to get her hair cut in week 6. I mean, it seemed like a good idea at the time, because it was taking so long to dry it every day, and I felt too rough to be bothered with it, but now that the nausea is easing off a bit, I've found that my hair *still* takes forever to dry, but now it also makes my face look like a potato. So that's just *fantastic*, really.)

(I'd probably go so far as to tell Pre-Pregnancy Me not to make *any* major decisions in the first trimester at all. Because they're all mostly morning-sickness driven, and hunched over a toilet isn't really a good place to be making major life plans, you know?)

Honestly, though, I may have crossed that invisible line in the sand, but I'm still struggling with the ol' imposter syndrome. Now that the nausea has started to settle down a little, there's really not much to reassure me that everything is still OK: there are still at least a few weeks to go until I can expect to feel movement, and although my bloat-bump can look fairly impressive, depending on the time of day, and what I'm wearing, it's not any bigger this week than it was last week, which leaves me with that whole, "Am I REALLY pregnant, or did I just eat too many bagels again?" feeling.

(This week's craving has been for bagels, by the way: so, yeah, I probably DID eat too many of them, to be perfectly honest...) On the subject of the bloat-bump, I thought it might be nice to celebrate the start of the second trimester by taking some photos of it, and what was weird about that was that, when I looked back at them, I immediately noticed that it wasn't actually my body in them. Like, it was my head (not looking its best, it has to be said, but still recognisably *my head)*, but with SOMEONE ELSE'S BODY attached to it. And yes, this was an ALL-CAPS kind of moment for me.

It's weird: I mean, I obviously knew I had a bump (even though I still think it's mostly bloat, on top of the pot belly I've always had...), and that my boobs were a bit "HELLO BOYS!" (I'm flattering myself wildly here: they're still a B-cup, but now they actually *fill* that b-cup, which is a novel experience, to be sure. Terry was all, "Geez, your boobs are busting out of that bra!" and I was just like, "Nah, that's just what a bra's *supposed* to look like, actually..."), but I hadn't realised I would also get pregnant in my butt, which is a bit of a bummer (boom boom! I'm here all week, folks!) because, guys, I AM PREGNANT IN MY BUTT. Or so it would appear, anyway.

So, I'm trying my best not to freak out about this, because I obviously know my body is going to change, and I've actually been looking forward to having a cute little bump – I guess I just didn't anticipate my entire *body* being the bump? Or not being able to get that new-this-year Vivien of Holloway top over my boobs. And honestly, I'm torn: part of me is kind of hoping the boobs stay this size, purely for the novelty value, but on the other hand, I *do* really like that top, which, admittedly, was always a bit snug on me.

Dilemma of the Week:

Should I buy the VoH top in a larger size? Answers on a postcard, but only if your answer is going to be, "Yes, Amber, you should totally buy the top, why is this even a question?"

One more questions for you, though: why are people in general so absolutely hell-bent on scaring the crap out of me by telling me every pregnancy-related horror story they can think of? Because, ever since we made the announcement, I've found myself having a number of conversations that have gone a bit like this:

ME: "I'm 13 weeks today! So relieved to be in the 2nd trimester, with a lower risk of miscarriage!"

THEM: "I wouldn't be so sure: I had a miscarriage at 15 weeks – let me tell you aaaaalll about it..."

or

ME: "I'm still really anxious about all of the things that could go wrong..."

THEM: "I'm not surprised: I thought my pregnancy was going really well, but then <insert hugely traumatic event of choice>"

or even relatively silly stuff, like:

ME: "I'm really worried about the hospital stay, so I'd appreciate it if everyone could avoid posting scary stories about hospital stays: thanks!"

THEM: "Here is my scary story about a hospital stay: you're welcome!"

So, obviously I'm exaggerating just a little here, but that's honestly how some of the responses I've had have come across to me, and there've been a few times this week where I've found myself scratching my head and thinking, "Why would you tell me that, other than to just terrify me?" (And, if so, *no need*, seriously: I'm totally good for terror over here, I really don't need any more of it...) (I also feel like a bit of an asshole for even thinking this, because, just a few months ago I was all, "People should be able to talk openly about miscarriage!" and now I'm all, "Er, not to *me* though, thanks!")

(I'm still thinking about that top, btw...)

Anyway, it looks like the theme for this week is, "OMG My Bump Has Disappeared Since Yesterday – Oh No, Wait, There

It Is!" The following events take place between 19:00 hours on Friday and 21:00 hours on Monday, and, even by my own admission, will make me sound crazier than even I thought was possible. But I think my levels of general craziness have been well established by now anyway, so here goes...

My bump disappeared.

And then it came back.

So, picture it: it's Friday night, I'm lying on the couch watching *Fear the Walking Dead*, and every time I happen to glance down, my view is basically BOOBS! and then BELLY! This is kind of strange, because HELLO, NOT MY BODY! but also quite reassuring as the presence of the bloat/bump is really the only evidence I have that there's something in there, as I can't feel any movement yet, even though people keep on telling me I totally should by now. That's a whole other story, trust me.

Anyway, fast-forward to roughly the same time on Sunday night. I'm lying on the couch, watching *Fear the Walking Dead* (this isn't Groundhog Day, by the way, it's just my life now), but *now* when I glance down, my view is basically BOOBS! and then NOTHING! Well, OK, not quite nothing – my belly is looking significantly flabbier than it used to, but what it does *not* look like any more, is a bump– and this freaks me out. Where did the baby go? Is it, like, hiding in my leg or something? Is that why my butt is so big? WHERE IS MY BUMP?

Now, I should add here that I'm not *totally* stupid. Like, I am *fairly* stupid, yes, but even I know that the first trimester "bump" is mostly just bloating (Which makes it even weirder for me when people want to touch it: I'm just like, 'Er, you do know that's just my lunch you're fondling, right?") so I guess it might make sense for that to go down sometimes? Maybe? Also, when I weighed myself on Sunday morning, I had lost a pound again (I've basically been losing and then regaining this same pound since the start of this pregnancy, with the result that now, at 13 weeks, I weigh exactly the same as I did before I even found out...) so I guess that might be why. Whatever the reason, though, I worried about it all day, and then on Monday night I... well, I lay down on the couch again to watch *Fear the Walking Dead* (Hey, did I mention we've been watching *Fear the Walking Dead*? Because we've been watching *Fear the Walking Dead*. We really need to get out more, huh?), and BAM – the bump was back!

I'm now trying to just accept that it's Not Actually a Real Bump at this stage, and that it's probably going to come and go due to bloating, but yeah, that was a very Not Fun 24 hours, with the worry compounded by the fact that the nausea has all but disappeared this week. I *should* be happy about this, obviously, but while I did know that a lot of people start to feel better in the 2nd trimester, I didn't expect to be one of them, and I really didn't expect it to disappear right at the very start of the 2nd trimester, so I was a bit thrown by that. With that said, I may not have a lot of nausea, but I have absolutely no appetite whatsoever. People keep saying, "But what would you *like* to eat, if you could have anything?" and I'm just like, "Nothing. I would like to eat nothing. If I could just somehow arrange to be given all of my nutrition in capsule form right now, that would suit me down to the ground."

(I *am* still eating, by the way, so no need to worry: I'm just not *enjoying* it. Which is a shame, really, because eating is normally one of my hobbies...)

I wonder what the bump will look like today?

Things I Would Like to Go Back in Time in Order to Tell My Pre-Pregnancy Self:

1. You will make it to the second trimester, and get to be one of those women with the cute little bumps, only sometimes you won't have a cute little bump, you'll have no bump at all, and that'll be weird, but OK.

2. Don't cut your hair. No, seriously: DO NOT CUT YOUR HAIR.

3. It's time to remove all social media from your phone, sister: it's the only way to stop people telling you their pregnancy-related horror stories.

4. You will survive the morning sickness. You will have no idea how you actually did it (Spoiler alert: it won't be ginger biscuits, though...), but I guess the good news is that constant nausea can't actually kill you: it'll just *feel* like it's going to.

5. By the time week 14 rolls around, you'll have forgotten all about that stupid top, so maybe just stop thinking about it now, and save yourself the trouble, hey?

Week 14
Kicking the Bucket,
Only Not Like *That*

As soon as I found out I was pregnant, I went out and bought a plastic bucket. (OK, it was really a bowl, but calling it a bowl wouldn't allow me to make that hilarious joke in the title of this diary entry, so...)

It was my first ever pregnancy-related purchase, and I get that it's a bit of an unusual one, but the thing is, and I'm guessing you've probably gathered this much by now, I was terrified of morning sickness. *Terrified.* I was mostly terrified of actually throwing up, obviously, but I am one of those people who only has to see vomit in order to start throwing up, so I was also fairly paranoid about throwing up in a place other than the bathroom, and ending up caught up in a helpless, never-ending cycle of vomiting, seeing the vomit, vomiting again, and so on and so forth, world without end.

In order to avoid this situation, I knew I'd have to make sure I always either:

a) Threw up directly into the toilet, keeping my eyes closed at all times.

b) Threw up into my trusty plastic bucket, which I could then just empty into the toilet, with my eyes closed.
Or

c) Threw up into some other receptacle, which I could then just dispose of. With my eyes closed, natch.

(My 2nd pregnancy-related purchase? Sick bags. Or 'Poorly Pouches' as they're oh-so-cutely called. I keep some in the car, and some in my handbag at all times. 'Be Prepared' is my motto. Well, that and 'Keep Your Eyes Closed While You're Throwing Up, Yo.')

So I bought me a bucket, and the bucket has lived next to my bed for almost three months now, apart from those times when I chose to descend to the living room or office, when the bucket would come with me, my faithful plastic companion. I even took it to my parents' house one time, even though I knew my mum would take its presence there as a slight upon her own sick bowl-providing abilities, and want to get me a bigger, *better* bowl of her own. And she did. (I'm pleased to report that I never actually had to use either the bowl or the sick bags, because I always managed to make it to the bathroom just in time, but just knowing they were there if necessary was a comfort to me...)

Anyway, today, at 14 weeks pregnant, I finally retired the sick bowl, taking it on its final (I hope) journey down to the kitchen, where it will now live out its days as just a regular bowl, with regular bowl duties. It will probably forget all about the time it spent as Sick-Bowl-in-Waiting, but I will never forget *it*, and that's the main thing, isn't it? From all of this you will gather that the nausea has finally started to recede. I mean, I'm pretty sure it'll make an instant comeback as soon as it knows the bowl is gone, but the fact that I currently feel confident enough to move around my house without the fear of throwing up at any second is a big improvement for me, so long may it continue.

In other news, everyone keeps telling me that, now that I'm in the 2nd trimester, I can expect my skin, hair and nails to all be totally *fabulous* now. Naturally, then, I woke up this morning with a giant zit on my forehead, for the first time in years. I have named it Trevor, and yesterday Trevor and I spent a few hours out shopping – my longest time on my feet and out of the house since May, basically. It was for a sponsored blog post but it was a lot of fun, and so good to feel like "myself" again, and just be out doing normal, non-pregnancy, non-anxiety-related things.

OK, I had a few little wobbles when I went into some of my favourite stores and realised that none of their clothes will fit me right now (and probably not *ever*, if everything I've been told about post-partumn body shapes is anything to go by...), but for the most part I felt absolutely fine – so much so that, when I got home, I went out into the garden and did some much-needed weeding, before collapsing in front of the TV and eating my way through the contents of the fridge, even although we'd just been out for lunch. I guess you could safely say the nausea has receded, then...

Of course, it didn't take long for the worry to set in, as I all-of-a-sudden realised that I felt totally NOT PREGNANT, and hey, you know who else feels NOT PREGNANT? PEOPLE WHO ARE NOT PREGNANT, that's who. And yes, yes: I know lots of people say they don't feel particularly pregnant during the 2nd trimester, but I really didn't think that would happen to me, and, if it did, I definitely didn't think it would be happening this soon. So, yeah, now I'm worrying about not feeling ill: SERIOUSLY, BODY.

Other than that, this week I think the reality of this pregnancy has really started to hit me, thus opening up a whole new world o'worry that has hitherto been unexplored. Until now, I've been so focused on all of the things that could go wrong, that I haven't really allowed myself to consider the possibility that things might go *right*, but now? Well, now I'm still very focused on all of the things that could go wrong, obviously, but I've also started to consider the possibility that, HOLY HELL, I MIGHT ACTUALLY HAVE TO PUSH A LIVE HUMAN OUT OF MY BODY, and won't that be fun? Not. And then, of course (Assuming I don't die in childbirth, which I almost certainly will...) I will then have a whole other human to look after. Forever. And *ever*. Which is scary, no?

I mean, setting aside for the moment the small, but important, fact that I don't have a clue how babies actually work, I keep thinking that one day that baby will be a child, and then a teenager (TEENAGERS SCARE ME), and then, finally, an adult. This raises all kinds of worries.

For instance:

- What if it doesn't like me? Plenty of people don't after all. What if my own child is one of them?

- What if I don't like it either?

- What if I do like it, but then, as soon as it's old enough, it's all, "Catch you later, mum, I'm off to live in Bali!"

- What if it marries a really bitchy girl, and *she* hates me, and I have to spend the rest of my life smiling sweetly at her while secretly wanting to stick pins in her eyes? WHAT IF?

So, basically, while other people who are 14 weeks pregnant probably spend their time reading lists of baby's names, and buying cute little outfits or something, here I am worrying about that ungrateful daughter-in-law of mine, what did I ever do to deserve such a child?

That, of course, is far from my biggest worry right now, though. I mean, it's a *big* worry, sure, but even worse is the fact that, now that I'm into the 2nd trimester, I've basically gone from having scans every two weeks, purely for reassurance (I've honestly got no idea how on earth that happened, but the Early Pregnancy Unit suggested it, and I was more than happy to go along with it...) to having absolutely nothing to reassure me at all, until my next appointment with my midwife, at 18 weeks.

I'm freaking out.

The biggest issue here is the fact that I feel absolutely fine right now. This is just one of the many ways in which pregnancy turns absolutely everything you know on its head, because, yes, I'm actually worried because I *don't* feel ill. I mean, how twisted is that, seriously?

It's true, though: I have no nausea, no aches and pains, and definitely no sign of movement or baby kicks. The question, then, is this: how the hell am I supposed to know whether this baby is still alive?

No, seriously, HOW? Because, just a few hours after the epic meltdown I had when I found out there would be no reassurance available for another four weeks - FOUR WEEKS, PEOPLE - a vague acquaintance insisted on telling me aaaaalll about the three stillborn babies her daughter had had. GOD.

From this, I learnt two things:

1. People are going to keep on telling me scary stories, no matter how many times I ask them not to. I'm still really surprised by this, because I'd assumed that common sense/basic social etiquette would dictate that people *not* say these things to pregnant women, but I'm quickly discovering that I'm pretty much alone in that assumption, which ... well, at least I know now, huh?

2. There is no end to the worry. As soon as I cross one bridge, I find another one right there waiting for me, so I've basically accepted now that I will worry until the end of the pregnancy, and then I'll worry about the baby itself. At least I've had a lot of practice in that area, though...

Week 15
Baby Brain

5 things I have done this week:

1. While speaking to my mum on the phone, I spent a good five minutes pacing around the ground floor of the house, searching for my phone. Which I was using at the time. GAH.

2. Had an absolutely hilarious story to tell you all as example: I have absolutely no idea what it was now. (It was really, really good, though: like, the best story ever, I swear. Please all just laugh politely...)

3. Spent at least 10 minutes staring at the blank screen of this diary entry, trying desperately to remember what example #2 was supposed to be.

4. Thought to myself, "Oooh, I must go and check that thing on the internet!" I still don't remember what "that thing on the internet" was, even although I went immediately to my computer to check whatever it was.

5. Had to write my address on a returns label. Wrote the address of the house I lived in almost four years ago, instead.

So, yeah, it's been that kind of week, really. Before I got pregnant, I used to hear people talk about "baby brain," and I'd just think, "Yeah, yeah, that totally doesn't sound like A Thing," but now... now I just can't even remember how I was planning to end this sentence, so maybe it is? Also, does anyone have even the slightest clue what I was talking about?

Also, what *was* that thing I went racing to my computer to Google, only to end up just looking at videos of cats on Facebook, instead? WHAT?!

(Also, AWWW, CATS!)

Oh, and I also ordered no less than five pairs of maternity jeans from GAP, only to end up sending them all back: it seems that most clothing manufacturers think that women get taller as well as rounder when they get pregnant, and while I really, really wish that was the case, nope, my legs are still as short as ever, unfortunately.

To be fair, there were a couple of pairs that could have worked, but they were *just OK*, and *I'm* NOT OK with spending money on clothes that are JUST OK these days – especially when I'm only going to be wearing them for a few months. I mean, I suspect I'm probably being a little bit overly-optimistic by expecting to find maternity jeans that are anything *other* than "OK", but I do have one pair which are nice, if a little too large at the moment, so I'm just going to hope I grow into them, and, if not, well there's always leggings, isn't there? Now there's a sentence I thought I'd never type.

Pregnancy-wise, there's really not much to report: I did have a bit of mild nausea back at the start of the week (Which served as a timely reminder of how absolutely awesome it is not to feel nauseous all the damn time: I swear I will never take that for granted ever, ever again...), but other than that, I'm still feeling very NOT PREGNANT... which is worrying, of course, but which everyone tells me is perfectly normal at this stage of pregnancy, so I'm just having to content myself with that.

This was, however, also the week that Terry's mum started chemotherapy, so that's obviously been occupying a large part of our minds. The update to this is that, having been given just 6 months to live by NHS Lothian, and told there was absolutely nothing that could be done (They even told us they didn't see much point in her doing chemo...), we managed to get a second opinion from a surgeon in London, who specialises in this type of cancer, and who feels that, although it can't really be *cured*, there is a possibility of surgery, which could drastically slow it down. That, however, depends on her having fairly aggressive chemo first, so she started that this week, and has, as is typical for Terry's mum, been an absolute trooper throughout. She's not been feeling too bad so far, but we're spending as much time with her as possible, so we can keep a close eye on her, and just keeping everything crossed that she responds well – I reckon we're about due some good luck around about now, no?

Week 16
Gas or baby, baby or gas?

So, the theme for this week is "there is no theme for this week". GOD.

Yup, it seems that week 15 flowed easily into week 16, the way weeks tend to do, and there's basically nothing much to tell me I'm pregnant right now: well, other than the giant bump that used be my midriff, obviously. Which means that, actually, I guess there is a theme for this week after all: the theme is, "Why the hell can't I feel movement yet, seriously, what is wrong with me?"

Now, I know, I know: the average time for women feeling movement is 17 – 21 weeks, and lots and lots of people have told me that I'm totally average in this respect, and that they didn't feel movement at 16 weeks either. For every person who tells me that, though, there's been at least 5 other people who could feel their babies blink right from the moment of conception, and WAH, why can't that be meeeeee? Because I don't WANT to be "average" right now: "average" is scaring the crap out of me, and making me worry, and then worry some more, and, actually, I would quite like to be an overachiever in this respect, thanks. Why can't I do that?

The main consequence of this uncertainty is a whole lot of anxiety, obviously. As proof of this, I present into evidence:

Things I Have Googled This Week:

"Is it a baby, or is it just gas?"

"Seriously, though, baby or gas????"

"Movements at 16 weeks: does it feel anything like gas?"

"Pictures of labradoodle puppies"

"People who didn't feel baby move at 16 weeks but everything turned out to be totally OK"

"Puppies and babies: really great idea"

"I think it's just gas, but could it actually be baby?"

"Can I just buy that Zara skirt one size up from my usual size, and it will fit me at 16 weeks pregnant but still fit me after the baby is born?"

"Babies and gas - virtually indistinguishable, really"

"How to stop your feet growing in pregnancy"

"How to afford replacements for all my shoes if my feet change size like everyone keeps telling me they will?"

"People who were totally sure it was just gas, but it was really the baby"

And so on and so forth.

(It was gas, btw. Don't ask me how I know...)

So, yeah, week 16 has seen a bit of an uptick in anxiety, and it's mostly due to the lack of reassurance that there's actually anything going on in there. Luckily I've managed to have my next midwife appointment moved to next week, instead of week 18, so I'm hoping Lovely Carolyn will be able to listen to the heartbeat and give me at least *some* reassurance then: other than that, it's just a countdown to the 20-week scan, which, in their infinite wisdom, our hospital have booked in for 21 weeks. They also booked my 12 week scan in for 13 weeks, and my 16 week midwife appointment for 18 weeks, so I feel a bit like they're just trying to taunt me now, and that, as soon as I get close to one of those milestones I've been chasing, they're just going to keep on moving it a little further away. We did manage to get the 12 week scan moved forward, though, so I'm hoping we can do the same with the 20 week one, but... yeah, not going to hold my breath, really.

Things I have worried about this week:

1. Eating ALL the things. It's strange, actually, because most of the time I'd say I don't really have much of an appetite, and I never really seem to feel hungry, as such, but then, as soon as I start eating, it's like the floodgates open and I can't seem to stop myself, until I've eaten half the house. This is actually worrying me a bit: not in a health-anxiety kind of way, just in a "wow, I'm going to be absolutely *huge* by the end of this, aren't I?" kind of way. I know you're not supposed to say that, because wanting to keep your figure is silly and frivolous, and all that, but, well, I guess I *am* silly and frivolous: WHO KNEW?

2. Sleeping positions. *I KNOW*. Who the hell is scared of SLEEPING POSITIONS? Er, this girl, that's who: ever since she read that she's only "allowed" to sleep on her left side, and never, ever on her back, otherwise the baby will die. SOOOO reassuring, no?

When I first read this, I actually felt quite smug, because I'd finally – FINALLY – found something I could be good at. I mean, I sleep on my left side anyway, always have, so I'd be able to just keep on doing what I'd always done, and get Brownie points for it: I win at pregnancy! Or, well, at this particular aspect of it, anyway. Of course, what I was totally forgetting here was that aspect of my personality which dictates that as soon as someone tells me I *have* to do something, I immediately want to do the complete opposite. So, pretty much the second I read the whole "left side only" thing, I immediately wanted to sleep on my *right* side, but only when I'm not sleeping on my back, which is what I really, really want.

So, I've obviously been trying my very best *not* to sleep on my back, obviously, because although the study that all of this scaremongering comes from doesn't seem particularly conclusive, I am very, very susceptible to scaremongering, and I've been well and truly *mongered* with this one. So every night, I dutifully lie on my left hand side, even though every nerve in my body is screaming, "RIGHT SIDE! RIGHT SIDE!" and then, what happens? Well, yesterday morning, I woke up flat on my back, with no memory of how I got there. After a quick freak-out, I rolled onto my left... and then woke up for the second time, a while later, happily curled up on my right. And now I feel like the worst person ever, because seriously, Amber, how hard can it be?

Anyway, I've given it a bit of thought, and the only solution I can come up with is to buy one of those weird body pillows pregnant women seem to love so much. I don't really want to get one of these, though, partly because I don't actually have any discomfort when I'm sleeping (yet), but mostly because they look huge, and I can't imagine how one would actually fit into our small double bed, without Terry having to vacate it first. Still, can you even claim to have experienced pregnancy if you haven't bought a pillow that's bigger than you are, and then told everyone how amazing it is? Because I don't think you can, really?

In other, much less frivolous news, Soula has started chemotherapy, and it turns out that chemotherapy is a real bitch, seriously. Of course, we're hoping chemotherapy will be the bitch that kicks the ass of the even-bigger-bitch that is cancer, and if it is, we'll thank it very much for that, but that's all well and good, and appropriately pep-talky, until you find yourself standing in a branch of TK Maxx, clutching the box you're planning to use to hold all of your baby/pregnancy memorabilia, and listening to your loved one sob down the phone, because she *just can't stop throwing up*, and she doesn't think she can do this any more, and then suddenly everything feels very bleak and hopeless, and very, very Not Good, and then you're looking at that baby box, and thinking that not all of the memories of this time are going to be good ones, are they? And how on earth are you supposed to deal with *that*?

Terry and I were in Edinburgh when all of this happened, but luckily his sister and brother were much closer, and, by the time we got there, Lila had already called the hospital, who'd told her just to bring her mum straight in. She was admitted that night, and spent the next two days in hospital: she's back home now, and feeling much better, but, of course, we're very aware that this was just round one, and there will be many more bouts to go before we'll even know if it's having the desired effect. So it's hard, and it's scary, and it's all kinds of awful, really, in ways I can't even begin to describe, but it's what we're dealing with right now, and I'm just glad that Soula is feeling better, and has so many people in her corner -as do we, of course. I have a feeling we're going to need them.

Week 17
Heartbeat

Guys, we have a heartbeat!

(Er, the title of this post kinda gave that away, didn't it? Now you know why my career as a suspense writer never took off...)

Hearing the baby's heartbeat at my midwife appointment this week was the culmination of 5 long weeks of some of the worst anxiety I've ever experienced in my life: and I say that as a veteran of kidney transplants (Terry's), ectopic pregnancies (Mine), and all sorts of other Very Bad Things.

It's been tough, folks.

To put it mildly.

I think a large part of the problem is that I still haven't felt any definite movement yet. I know that's totally normal, but people keep on excitedly asking if I can feel the baby move yet, and then recoiling in horror when I say no, and on Tuesday morning I opened up Twitter and the first thing I saw was a conversation between two people at roughly the same stage as me, talking about how awesome it is to feel those baby kicks, so... yeah. No matter how much you read about the "average" time for people to feel movement, it's hard (read: impossible) not to compare yourself to other people, and end up thinking, "WTF is wrong with me?" Or it is for me, anyway – and I'm not just talking about pregnancy, either.

But anyway!

Yesterday morning I had my latest midwife appointment. I was super-anxious going into this: not just because I knew she'd be listening to the heartbeat, and I was terrified it wouldn't be there, but also because I'd gotten it into my head that there would also be another blood test involved, and all of the recent cancer-related medical experiences we've had have really triggered my health anxiety, so I was basically convinced that I'd be spending the next few days waiting on bad news. More so than usual, I mean.

Well, there was no blood test: phew!

There was, however, a student in the room: GAH.

As soon as I laid eyes on her, sitting in the corner like a Dementor, my heart sank. This actually happened to me once before, at a counselling appointment, and honestly, having to pour out my innermost thoughts and deepest fears in front of an openly hostile teenager was one of the reasons I never went back. I get that students have to be trained, but it's hard enough for me to discuss medical issues with *one* person, let alone having to do it in front of an obviously bored audience (Actually, my mum tells me I was *born* in front of an audience, so you'd think I'd be used to it: one of her last memories as they wheeled her into surgery was of someone calling out, "Hey, anyone want to see a C-section?!"), you know?

It seems, however, that this is to be my fate, so I had to not only expose my deepest, darkest fears (plus my palest, palest stomach) in front of yet another surly teenager, I also had to sheepishly hand over a tube of urine in front of one, too. It was a real 'Dear Diary' moment, to be sure, especially given that, just like the last time, the student, a) Looked about 15 years old (I'm seriously not exaggerating, either: these look more like high school students than medical students to me, and they behave like it, too...), and b) Obviously just hated her life, and thought it was, like, SO UNFAIR that she was having to sit in a doctor's office on a nice summer's day, listening to some idiot of a woman drone about about her health anxiety.

To prove it, she sat with her shoulders slumped, glowering at me the whole time as if it was ALL MY FAULT and I had TOTALLY RUINED HER LIFE, and I know this is totally ridiculous, but by the time we left, I felt so, so stupid that I kind of wanted to cry a bit. (On the plus side, I guess it was all good practice for when the baby's a teenager, so there's that...)

I didn't, though, because as I said at the start of this post (Hey, remember the start of this post? I just about do...)...

We heard the heartbeat!

It was very loud, and very strong, and OMG guys, there is an actual baby in there! Like, a real, live baby! It's not just all of those mashed potatoes I've been eating! And, no, none of the various aches and pains I've had over the last few weeks have been a sign of something catastrophic happening – phew! It was all very emotional and exciting, but, because my surly teenage audience was looking particularly pissed off at that point, I felt I had to be all British about it, so, rather than leaping up and punching the air, which is what I wanted to do, I just kind of lay there, going, "Well, isn't that just *marvellous*?!" and other things that totally didn't sound like me.

I did buy a cake afterwards, to celebrate, though: and I will definitely request that there be no teenagers in the room for my next appointment, in a few weeks time, even though I know that makes me a terrible, terrible person, who is hampering the NHS in its bid to educate young minds... or whatever it thinks it's achieving by allowing bored teenagers to roll their eyes at pregnant ladies.

Things I Have Worried About This Week:

You'd think that hearing the heartbeat so clearly would have totally put my mind and rest, and allowed me to finally relax and just enjoy the rest of this pregnancy, but if you'd think that, then all I can say is that you've obviously never suffered from anxiety, because that's just not how it works, unfortunately.

Hearing the heartbeat reassured me for... as long as we were listening to the heartbeat, basically. As soon as Lovely Caroline removed the doppler from my stomach, and the thumping stopped, I was back to worrying again: because, OK, I know the heart was beating a few seconds ago, but what about NOW? How do I know it's still going? How do I know it won't just stop?

And this, I suspect, will just be my life from now on. Even although the spotting I had in the first week of pregnancy has never been repeated, for instance, I still look for it every time I go to the bathroom: which means that my bathroom is now the scariest place in the world, as far as I'm concerned, with every trip there leaving me a nervous wreck. Which is particularly inconvenient, really, given that, like most women in their 2nd trimester, I'm there so often these days that it would probably be easier for me to just move in.

Other than the ongoing knicker watch, the newest entry to the worry files this week is the state of the bumpy, bumpy roads where we live. You don't really realise *quite* how bumpy roads are until you're pregnant, and while I'm *pretty sure* I *can* drive over a speed bump without, like, having the baby just drop out of my body or something, I bet I'm not the first person to wonder if that's possible.

OR *AM* I?

Week 18
All Quiet

Until the day I found out I was pregnant, almost everything I knew about pregnancy came from soap operas – which, it turns out, are not actually all that accurate: who knew?

For instance, I'd been led to believe that the first symptom of pregnancy was... fainting. Yup, in Neighbours, if a female character faints, you can guarantee that she's pregnant – to the extent that, if I ever hear of someone fainting in real life, I now just immediately assume they're pregnant. Even if they're male.

The next symptom, of course, is morning sickness – which, in soap operas, only ever happens once, thus allowing the character to find out about the pregnancy, and then move on to more interesting plot lines. Now, I knew that part (the, "it happens once, and then never again," bit) wasn't true, and I'd also kind of figured out that some of the other stuff I'd learned about pregnancy from Neighbours *probably* weren't all that accurate either.

I'm talking about things like:

The way soap-opera pregnancies only last 3 months, if that. And if you're thinking that sounds pretty good, don't, because:

The baby will be at least 6 months old when it's born. Like, it will practically walk out of the womb and cut its own cord, seriously.

Once born, you will not have to see the baby again until it's old enough to have some interesting plot points. The only exception to this is if the baby is born with a life-threatening disease (which it will be), or manages to swallow poison, or be kidnapped. Which, again, *highly likely*.

In other words, I was woefully unprepared for the reality of pregnancy, but one of the things that has surprised me most about it - and I mean rocked me to my absolute core - is the fact that, now that I'm well into the 2nd trimester, being pregnant really doesn't feel all that different from... well, NOT being pregnant, really.

I mean, there are some differences, obviously, with the size of my belly being the main one. There's also been some - how can I put this delicately? - changes in the constitution, shall we say? This has actually come as a bit of a shock to me, because one of the ironies of my health anxiety is that despite perpetually thinking that I'm dying, I'm actually one of the healthiest people I know, and I rarely suffer from a lot of the things other people seem to get. (My first midwife appointment was actually quicker than it would usually have been, because when she started going through my medical history, I was able to say, "Well, I'm complete basket case, so there's *that*, but I'm not allergic to anything, I'm not on any medication and I don't have any health conditions: can I leave now?") Until I got pregnant, I'd hear people say things like, "Oh, I can't eat that: it gives me heartburn/indigestion/whatever," and I honestly didn't really have much of a concept of what those things even felt like, because, for the most part, I eat things, my body processes them, the end.

Well, I KNOW NOW, is all I'm saying, because from almost the second I found out I was pregnant, my body completely freaked out and forgot everything it ever knew. So now I eat something – anything, really – and my body's just like, "WHOA, there! I have NO IDEA what I'm supposed to do with this!" So I spend around 90% of my time in a lot of discomfort, and the other 10% grudgingly eating things that I know will cause me a lot of discomfort later.

So I guess if I were to sum up the first trimester, I would probably say, "A LOT OF DISCOMFORT. Also: *nausea*." I've basically spent the last 18 weeks trying unsuccessfully to digest my food. That's my life now. So, if someone asks me to do something now, I have to say, "Sorry, I can't, I'll be digesting my dinner that day: and the next, actually."

This week, however, has been so spectacularly uneventful that, if it wasn't for the crippling anxiety, and digestion fun, I'd have almost been able to convince myself that everything was totally normal, and that I didn't have an entire person currently stuck inside my body, and, OMG, how is it going to get out? HOW?

I was actually hoping this week *wouldn't* be uneventful, of course. I mean, I *was* hoping I'd have lots of lovely little baby kicks to report in this week's pregnancy diary, but nope: absolutely nada. Well, other than that one time during *Game of Thrones* when I became absolutely convinced I could feel ... *something*. Some kind of... *feeling*. It wasn't anything like a butterfly flapping its wings, though, which is what everyone and their uncle has told me to expect, and later that night I had a similar feeling way up in my torso, and if the baby is all the way up *there* then, well, I'm in trouble, basically.

So, yeah, nothing to report again, and I'm honestly starting to think that I will just *never* feel this baby move, *ever*. Why'd you hate me, baby? Why can't you just give me a swift kick to the belly or something, just so I know I haven't imagined you? Here's what I *do* have to report this week...

Zits. Four of 'em. Actually, I don't know if this has anything to do with pregnancy, because we all know that sometimes bad skin happens to good people, whether they're pregnant or not, but I don't *normally* get breakouts, so I'm chalking it up to hormones, and just feeling lucky that they cleared up almost as soon as they got here.

(Other things I'm chalking up to hormones: all of the times I've started crying just because someone looked at me funny; my continued inability to stay awake past 10pm...)

Oh, and the dreams! Super-vivid dreams were one of my very first pregnancy symptoms, and they've stayed with me throughout. Most of them seem to revolve around me breaking into my childhood home (Which I only lived in until I was 5 years old, but dream about constantly...), and then refusing to leave it, but quite a lot of them involve me endlessly re-sizing images for blog posts which... well, which says a lot about how I've been spending MY time lately, huh?

Things I Have Worried About This Week:

Other than the usual "why no movement?" stuff, this week I've mostly been worrying about the mid-pregnancy anomaly scan, which is happening next week. I stupidly made the mistake of Googling this, just so I'd know what to expect, and, of course, it was just this huge list of Things That Could Go Wrong. Well, OK, 11 things, and two of them have already been ruled out by the Harmony Test I had in week 10, but even so, folks, that's still nine different things that could potentially be wrong with this baby, and that's just TOO MANY THINGS, as far as I'm concerned.]

Still, if all goes well, that scan will be another one of those lines in the sand that, once crossed, should make me feel a whole lot better, so as much as I'm dreading it, I'm also looking forward to getting past that particular hurdle – and, of course, to (hopefully) finding out whether we're having a boy or a girl: by which I mean, "Having it confirmed that we're definitely having a boy, because we are definitely having a boy, and I know it."

Week 19
The Shifting

Well, it's my week 19 pregnancy update, folks, and the big news from this week was, of course, the mid-pregnancy anomaly scan – which I actually had at 19 weeks and 4 days (As opposed to the 20 weeks most people have it at, or the 21 weeks I'd been booked in for…), purely because I'm a special snowflake, in an, "I can't possibly wait another two weeks to see this baby," kinda way, so the hospital very kindly moved it forward for me. Thanks, hospital!

So! We got to see the baby! And We found out, not only that it's a boy, (TOLD YOU SO)but also that it's a very healthy little boy, who's developing exactly as he should be: I am so proud. I'm not gonna lie, though: I was an absolute mess going into this scan – as in, I didn't think I was going to be able to get out of the car when we got to the hospital, I was shaking so badly with nerves. This was my first scan in almost 8 weeks , and I. Was. Terrified. I was absolutely convinced I'd be told something was wrong, but happily the only thing "wrong" was my conviction that *something would be wrong*, and I was very happy about that indeed.

I was also worried about the scan because I'd read/heard that the sonographer would show us the baby briefly, and then turn the screen away and sit there in silence, while she looked at all of the Very Important Things they have to check, and I knew I'd be an absolute wreck while that was happening. Luckily for us, though, that turned out not to be the case, and instead she talked us through everything she was doing/looking at, which was all incredibly cool and detailed, and kind of mind-blowing really.

The sonographer also told me my placenta is right at the front, which she said will muffle movement from the baby, and make it unlikely that I'd be feeling much yet: so, it's not that he isn't moving, as I'd assumed, it's just that I can't feel it. With that said, this week I think I *might* be starting to feel something: I've been a little bit confused about this, though, because it doesn't feel like a butterfly flapping its wings, or like bubbles bursting, which is what everyone else seems to describe. It doesn't feel like gas, though, either, which is what makes me suspect it just *might* be some movement, although it's very subtle and sporadic, and some days I don't really feel anything at all. Hmm.

"But what DOES it feel like?" Terry asked when I told him this. And honestly? I don't really know how to describe it, other than by saying, "Well, it feels a bit like there's something in my belly which is moving very slightly from time to time..." I call it 'The Shifting'. Which, yes, makes this pregnancy sound a bit like a Stephen King novel or something, but, then again, when you suffer from anxiety, pregnancy *is* a bit like a Stephen King novel, isn't it? Like, if you were pitching a novel idea to someone who didn't know how pregnancy worked, and you were all, "So, it's about this person, yeah, who has *another person living inside them...*" the person you were pitching to would just be like, "Nah, dude, that's WAY too far-fetched and creepy: no one will *ever* believe that one!"

So, yes, The Shifting: I've been calling it that because it's just been this very subtle *shifting* sensation, which I'm only really aware of if I'm sitting still, or – slightly bizarrely – watching *Game of Thrones*. I dunno if the baby likes GoT or hates it, but he does seem to want to dance while it's on, so he's going to be pissed that he missed The Red Wedding, isn't he? We'll maybe leave that one until he's older, though...

Things I Have Worried About This Week:
Skin tags.

Well, ONE skin tag... which I obviously assumed was actually skin cancer, because, *health anxiety*. Well, I completely and utterly freaked out – we're talking full-on ugly crying, punctuated every few seconds by me rushing to the mirror to check it was still there, the works. I only calmed down when a quick look back through my blog photos revealed that, actually, I've ALWAYS had that skin tag, it's just gotten a little bit bigger, which obviously had me sounding the 'Skin Cancer' klaxon, but which is apparently very common in pregnancy, so I can stand down the vigil, apparently.

Some of this freak out was down to health anxiety/pregnancy hormones, obviously, but a large part of it was really down to everything that's been happening with Terry's mum lately, which has obviously been very triggering, as well as being just plain ol' awful, really. She was admitted to hospital again this week, and is still there: it's been a real blow, as she'd been dealing really well with her second round of chemo until then, and we were hoping she was past the worst of it with this cycle.

She was, however, thrilled to hear our news from the scan (As were my parents, who had to be restrained from rushing out and buying baby stuff: you can see where I get it from, can't you?) and, was also happy to hear that her uncanny ability to predict the sex of a baby by looking at the mother's backside has, once again, been proved correct.

(True story: for as long as I've known her, I've thought Soula was claiming to be able to predict the sex of a baby by looking at the mother's bump. This week I realised she's actually been saying "*bum*" (Soula is Greek: this kind of thing happens a lot. In fact, we all still fall about laughing every time she tells us she's going to go and put "a fresh shit" on the bed...). "You're definitely having a boy," she told me last week, "Because you got a bum now, and you no used to have a bum." (Please read that in a Greek accent to get the full effect.) Then she grabbed the offending bum. And we were walking down a public street at the time! My nephew Jonathan suggested I call this post, "My Mother-in-Law Groped My Ass," for this reason. Honestly, I did consider it...)

(Gotta admit, I'm now really curious to know what else my butt knows that I don't: ah, if butts could talk, the secrets they could tell!)

This week has also guest starred:

Crazy hormones.

Oh, hey, did I mention my hormones have been CRAZY this week? Because my hormones have been crazy this week – and not just during the whole 'Skin Tag' scare, either. I can basically burst into tears over just about anything right now, which has been tons o'fun for Terry, who's spent a lot of this week going, "But WHY are you crying?" only for me to reply, "I don't knoooowwww!" Fun times, indeed.

A really weird thing:

Also… I hesitate to even mention this, because it's kinda embarrassing, but on Tuesday morning I was doing my makeup and I discovered an inch-long white hair growing out of my forehead. My *forehead*. THE HELL KIND OF SORCERY IS THIS??!

Things I Have Worried About This Week:

My big fear this week was about the 20-week scan, but once I'd gotten through that, I managed to relax a bit. I AM, however, constantly still monitoring my belly for signs (well, *feelings*, rather…) of movement, and am a bit worried that my health anxiety/OCD is rapidly turning this into A Thing, and that, now that I've felt definite movement, I'll basically just have to give up my life, so I can count kicks all day instead. I've already woken up this morning and thought, "Hmm, I felt The Shifting last night: why no Shifting this morning?" and even though I know perfectly well that I'm not going to feel movement ALL the time, I can already tell that this particular saga is set to run and run.

Looks like the next few months are going to be fun, huh?

Week 20
Halfway There

(If your mind didn't just automatically add the words, "We're livin' on a prayer," to that headline, then I don't even know how to relate to you, sorry...)

Big news, folks:

I felt the baby kick!

As in, actually *kick*: not bubbles, or butterfly wings flapping, or even a subtle shifting. No, this was an unmistakable kick, which I felt, not just in my belly, but also on my hand, which happened to be resting on said belly at the time. It felt so freaky that I instantly snatched my hand away, and then burst out laughing when I realised what it was. There was absolutely no doubt that it was a kick, though, so unless there's something *else* inside me that can do that, let the record show that, as of midnight at the very start of week 20, WE HAVE MOVEMENT, PEOPLE: THIS IS NOT A DRILL.)

I was happy for at least five minutes: euphoric, in fact. Then the downwards spiral began...

So, it's 8am on Saturday morning. I've just eaten a bar of chocolate, and now I'm lying in bed with my phone pressed to my belly, blasting Taylor Swift to my unborn child, in a bid to make it move. Suddenly, it hits me (Not the baby, a realisation): this is *it*, isn't it? This is what madness feels like, and it's all going to be downhill from here. There's a glass of water chilling in the fridge (Because if the chocolate and music don't work, I'm told that ice cold water will...), the midwife is about to be woken up with a panicked phone call, and I've officially arrived in Crazytown.

I'm scared because I felt the baby move this time yesterday morning, but I haven't felt it since then, and I have no idea whether that's normal or not. And this is the problem for us first-timers, isn't it?

They tell you the baby will develop a pattern of movement... but they don't tell you when that will happen. I only started feeling movement a few days ago: should the pattern have established itself by now, or is it still too early? WHO KNOWS.

They tell you that if you haven't felt movement in a while, you should eat some chocolate... but they don't tell you how *much* to eat, or how soon afterwards you should expect to feel movement. Ditto the ice cold water.

They tell you that if these techniques fail, you should call your midwife... but, again, they don't tell you at what stage you even need be worrying about this stuff anyway. I've heard some people say that movement doesn't become consistent until later in pregnancy, but then again, I've heard other people say that any change *at all* is a cause for huge concern. I've been told that those of us with anterior placentas will feel movement later, and that it will be "muffled" by the placenta at first... but I've also been told by people *with* anterior placentas that it doesn't make the slightest difference, and that *they've* been able to feel their babies move from the moment of conception: so what's wrong with me, then?

And this is the question that's been rolling around in my head for this entire pregnancy now: WHAT'S WRONG WITH *ME*? Why do I seem to be so different from everyone else, even though all of the stats, and all of the medical professionals I've seen, tell me that, actually, I'm completely average?

I don't *feel* average, though. I feel far, far below average, in just about every respect. Not only did I feel movement so much later than everyone else seems to, I also apparently weigh SO MUCH MORE than everyone else does at my stage, too. Last week I posted a photo on Instagram (Which I later deleted, because I decided I hated it: <insert eyeroll emoji>) and mentioned in the caption that I was bored with maternity wear already: almost immediately, I started getting comments from people who were amazed that I was having to buy it *at all,* and who wanted me to know that *they* didn't buy *any* maternity clothes, because *they* were just *so teeny-tiny* all the way through their pregnancies that they didn't even need it.

My first reaction to these comments was to feel a bit depressed to think that, even in pregnancy, being thin is still seen as the normal and desirable way to be. My second reaction, meanwhile, was, "WHAT'S WRONG WITH *ME*?" Why can't I leave my house without someone telling me how HYYYOOOOOGGGEE I am, while people who are about to give birth any day are apparently still wearing their normal clothes, and complaining about how loose everything is on them?

(To be fair, I did get one comment on that post from someone telling me I should just give up on clothes altogether, because by the end of the pregnancy not even maternity wear will fit me, and I'll have to buy an adult onesie. Which was depressing in a different kind of way...)

I know that this is ridiculous, obviously. I know perfectly well that every pregnancy is different, and that there's absolutely nothing to be gained by comparing myself to other people, but, at the same time, I feel like I'm constantly being invited to do exactly that: either by people who want me to know how much *thinner* than me they are/were, or by people comparing me to some idea they have in their head of what a pregnant woman should look like at this stage (Answer: NOT LIKE ME, apparently...). I know I'm being silly, but the frequency of the comments, combined with the shocked tone in which they're always uttered, makes me feel once more like the odd one out, even though I know I'm *not.*

Speaking of being the odd one out: none of the supposedly failsafe methods of getting the baby to move worked for me (Just as none of the tried-and-tested ways to stop morning sickness ever worked for me either...), but, that afternoon, the baby started moving, and basically didn't stop for rest of the day. Then the next day? Hardly anything. The day after that, he was super-active again, and that's been my week, basically:

constantly monitoring movements without knowing what counts as "normal" at this stage, and worrying that if there isn't any kind of pattern to those movements (Other than the "tons of movement one day, very little the next," one), then how will I know if something's wrong?

Things Everyone Tells You Will Definitely, Absolutely, With 100% Certainty, Make Your Baby Kick:

- Hot drinks
- Cold drinks
- Sugary snacks
- Jumping Jacks
- Loud music
- Lying on your side

Things That Make MY Baby Kick:

- The baby deciding to kick.

I mean, is it any wonder I'm a complete basket case right now?

Week 21
More Milestones

This week, I somehow reached a totally unanticipated point in my pregnancy where I've almost lost track of which stage I'm at.

Seriously, I did *not* see this coming. In the first trimester, you (And by "you" I mean "me") track your progress in days as well as weeks: sometimes even in *hours*, if I'm honest. After that, I calmed down a little, and just started thinking of myself as being "14 weeks", say, rather than, "14 weeks, 3 days and 11 hours." Now, though? Now I'm having to pause for a second whenever someone asks me how far along I am, so I can go, "20 weeks... oh no, wait! 21 weeks... I think!"

I am still counting in weeks, rather than months, though, obviously. Before I was pregnant, I used to inwardly eye-roll a bit when I'd ask someone how old their kid was, and they'd go, "He's 172 weeks!" I mean, COME ON, people, give me a number that actually means something to me, here! Now, though, I have learned the error of my ways: there may not be a huge difference from week to week right now, but each one is still a major milestone for me... even when I forget to count them.

Speaking of milestones, we had a pretty good one this week:

Terry got to feel the baby move!

I was sitting on the couch on Sunday night when I started to feel him (the baby, I mean, not Terry...) move around a bit, so I quickly grabbed Terry's hand, placed it on my belly, and within a few seconds he'd felt a little... "kick" seems like too strong a word for what I'm feeling at the moment, so I'm going to go with "nudge" instead. So, he felt a nudge. It was a nice nudge, though, and he's had another one since then, as has my mum, who found it a little bit awkward having to essentially put her hand down my jeans (Well, the baby was pretty low that night, and those maternity waistbands are hiiiiigh...) to feel it, but who tells me it was totally worth it.

As for me, meanwhile, I'm *also* being nudged on a regular basis, although the baby still seems to be stuck in that pattern where he moves loads one day, and then hardly at all the next, which means I'm still spending every second day in a mess of anxiety – fun for all the family, really!

The other highlight of the week was getting to hear the baby's heartbeat again at my latest appointment with the midwife. I asked Terry to record the audio on my phone, so we could let our parents hear it, but instead he decided to film a video of me looking like a very sweaty, anxious, Jabba the Hut – one for the memory book, for sure.

Other than that, the appointment was uneventful: thankfully the midwife reassured me that the on/off pattern of movement I've been having is totally normal at this stage, which helped reassure me a bit, especially as the appointment came right after a day of high anxiety, in which I'd hardly felt anything until I went to bed, at which point he'd decided that now was the time to be gettin' busy in there. (Not complaining at all by the way: he can kick me as much as he likes, if that's what it takes to let me know he's still there!)

This week we've also started to think about some of the baby-related purchases we need to make before he arrives. This is actually a really big deal for me, because my anxiety still won't even allow me to save a piece of maternity clothing to my ASOS watch list (Because that would just be tempting fate, wouldn't it?), so the thought of actually buying a pram, say, or a cot, makes my stomach churn with anxiety. Or it could just be The Shifting: it's hard to tell these days.

With all of that said I did buy a pair of maternity trousers, and, OK, also a sweater, as well as picking up a few more basics in the Gap sale, but I AM NOT ON TRIAL HERE, PEOPLE.

GOD.), but I have started to freak out a bit (Like, a really, really big bit....) about everything we need to do/buy for the house before the baby arrives.

I know first babies rarely arrive early (or even on time, for that matter. I myself was 10 days late, for instance. Well, I always have enjoyed a lie in...), but I actually know quite a few people whose first babies did arrive very early, so this week I got into a bit of a panic, which was only stopped in its tracks when Terry agreed to sit down with me and write a list of Very Important Things That Absolutely Need to Be Done, And Need to Be Done NOW. God, I love a list. I feel like just HAVING a list makes you feel instantly productive, you know?

Top of the list? We need to build a shed. Yes. I know that's not what pregnant women are normally most concerned about, but I really, really need this shed, and I need the shed so we can clear out the cupboard under the stairs... which, actually, is not so much a "cupboard" right now as it is a Black Hole of Doom, the door of which I'm terrified to open in case the contents just come spilling out and swallow me whole. You know that episode of *Friends* where it's revealed that neat-freak Monica has a Cupboard Of Shame, which is crammed full o'crap? It's like that, basically. And it needs to NOT be like that for very much longer, because it's where we're planning to store things like a pram/stroller and various other bits of baby-related equipment that we probably don't even know we need yet. In its current condition, we literally couldn't get ONE MORE THING into that cupboard, and I'm honestly not joking about being scared to open the door, so a clear-out needs to happen, and the sooner the better.

Before we can do that, though, we need to build that shed, so that all of the things that are currently residing in the cupboard under the stairs can live, instead, in the shed. We've actually been trying to sort this out for months now, because this is something we wanted to have done regardless of the imminent arrival of a small person with a huge amount of associated equipment, but we've been let down a few times so far: GOD.

LIKE, HOW HARD IS IT TO HAVE A SHED BUILT, SERIOUSLY?!

We've currently been promised (By a contractor I will henceforth refer to simply as Shed Man...) that the shed will be in situ by the end of September. I have my doubts about that happening, really, but I've just written two entire paragraphs about a stupid SHED, of all things, so I'm going to shut up now and think about what my life has become. I mean, SERIOUSLY.

Things I Have Worried About This Week That Are Not Shed-Related:

Despite nothing of note happening this week, pregnancy-wise, it's actually been a pretty bad one in terms of anxiety. No particular reason for this (other than that on/off pattern of movement): I just find that, the more time goes on, the more I obsess over all the things that could go wrong, so my anxiety has been sky-high lately, even though I know I should be feeling pretty calm. Even just writing this post makes me feel oddly guilty, because I keep thinking, "Why I am I writing about nurseries and maternity trousers, and, well, *sheds*, when something could be about to go wrong at ANY second?" I know that's not rational, but neither is health anxiety, and it's really had me in its grips this week. The swine.

The good(ish) news here is that I have an appointment with my consultant in a couple of weeks: this is mostly to discuss my fears about childbirth and hospitalisation, but the midwife has referred me for perinatal counselling, and is also arranging for me to speak to someone about hypnobirthing. This actually kind of worries me as my issues are all about control, and the word "hypnosis" kind of implies the complete *opposite* of that, although I'm assured it's nothing like what I'm imagining (Me on a stage being told to dance like a chicken or something, and being unable to stop myself blindly obeying, basically...), and could actually help me feel more in control.

I'm not generally a fan of any kind of mindfulness/meditation type stuff because I find I'm just far too impatient to actually get through it (Yoga, for instance, is always really stressful for me, because I find it so boring my mind just starts racing through all of the things it thinks it *should* be doing instead. With mindfulness, meanwhile, I've yet to finish reading a full page about it, because my non-mindful mind just starts wandering. It wandered while I was writing that sentence, actually: what was I talking about again?), but I'm more than happy to hear what they have to say about it, and will keep an open mind (probably *so* open that every thought will leave as fast as it arrived, knowing me, but I can but try...): as I said to the midwife, anything that can help make all of this easier for me is very welcome right now...

Week 22
The Pressure to be Perfect

What can I tell you about week 22?

Er, other than the usual, "Sometimes the baby moves a LOT, and it's awesome, but other times he doesn't seem to move much at all, which is terrifying," stuff that I usually write in these updates, I mean?

When he moves, I feel amazed and relieved – and also just a *little* bit freaked out, if I'm honest. The movements, when they come, are much stronger now, and if I place my hand on my belly I can literally feel him wriggling around in there, which makes me alternate between howling with laughter (I've no idea why I find it so amusing, I just do...) and thinking, "OMG, there's something LIVING IN MY BELLY, WHAT EVEN?!" I dunno, it just makes it all so real, somehow, in a way that even seeing it on the scan doesn't come close to. I guess when you see the scan, you're looking at a computer screen, which makes it easier to view this little being that's moving around as being totally unconnected to *you*, if that makes sense? When it's 1am, and he decides to start dancing, though, that's a totally different feeling, and, WHOA, is it ever strange. *Good* strange... but strange.

So, when he moves, I'm happy... and when he doesn't move, I feel like the anxiety is probably going to kill me. Which has been the pattern of this week, and pretty much *every* week in the second trimester, really. Gulp.

A couple of other things happened this week to increase my anxiety even more, though:

Thing the 1st:

I bought a face cream with retinol in it. You are *not* supposed to use face creams with retinol in them. But I didn't know that, so I bought it, and I used it (only around 5 times, but still...), and when I found out that it was on the FORBIDDEN list, I just about died, seriously. In my defence, there was nothing on the box or bottle to say that the thing shouldn't be used in pregnancy. Honestly, though, I just wasn't thinking: it didn't even occur to me that something I put on my face might have an effect on my unborn child: I obviously realise that it probably *should* have occurred to me, but, of course, hindsight is 20-20, and I am not perfect, as much as I wish I was.

Having done some frantic Googling on the subject, I feel a little better about it: it seems like there's really very little risk at all with this kind of thing, but the problem with these endless lists of Things Thou Shalt Not Do When Pregnant is that they have a way of breeding guilt and paranoia, which can quickly take over your life. Speaking of which...

Thing the 2nd:

People keep on telling me I shouldn't be sitting with my legs or ankles crossed: I keep on doing it. This week I was (YET AGAIN) gently reminded that this is on the Forbidden list, and (YET AGAIN) I felt like an absolute idiot for having to constantly be reminded about it. And, I mean, it seems like this should be easy, right? Like, just stop crossing your legs, Amber, FFS. It seems, however, that crossing my legs is completely habitual for me: I do it without even thinking about it, and even when I consciously try to stop myself from doing it, my good intentions only last as long as it takes for my mind to be occupied by something else, and those legs are crossed again before I know it. Dammit.

Now, I wasn't able to find any definitive medical evidence to support the idea that it's dangerous for pregnant women to cross their legs, although I did find a lot of anecdotal "evidence", plus quite a few people's grannies telling them it makes the umbilical cord wrap around the baby's neck... so I guess that IS pretty definitive, then? Whether it's true or not, however, the fact that people keep on scolding me (however gently) for doing it has made me feel guilty and paranoid, to the point that I've spent the entire week obsessing over the position of my legs, and am currently typing this with them propped uncomfortably in front of me, in a bid to stop them crossing.

(I just Googled it again while writing this post, and came across a page which informed me that there is a correct way for pregnant women to sit, stand, drive, and I gave up reading at that point because I was too busy trying to make sure my earlobes were in line with my shoulders...)

Seriously, can you even believe I just typed two full paragraphs about something as banal as my leg position? I can't. But this is my life now: and when you're constantly being told that you shouldn't do this, that, or the next thing, it becomes hard *not* to worry, or to feel like every single thing you do has the potential to cause harm. I mean, if this baby's health really *does* depend on me being absolutely *perfect* in every way – never crossing my legs, never sleeping on my right hand side, never eating thing from the Forbidden List, never using a new beauty product without first of all calling my GP to make sure it's OK – then it really is doomed, isn't it?

(Also, do people actually go to their GP to check they can use face creams? Because even some of the products that do claim to be safe for use will have a little disclaimer somewhere on the box, saying that if you're pregnant or breastfeeding, you should consult your doctor before using them, and I can't even imagine the response I would get if I took up my GP's time to ask him about that new eye cream that arrived in the post last week...)

That's obviously not true, though, is it? And, despite my paranoia, I don't *really* believe my baby will die just because I crossed my ankles occasionally. I do, however, feel that society in general puts a lot of pressure on pregnant women, and really encourages them to feel that they're constantly in danger of causing irreparable harm by doing something they didn't think twice about. Honestly, some days I feel like the safest thing would be to just stay in bed for the next few months, so I can stay out of trouble, but, of course, sleeping seems to be the most dangerous thing of all (I'm still finding myself rolling onto my back at times, although the giant pregnancy pillow I finally got round to buying has helped with that...), so maybe not.

In other week 22 pregnancy news, meanwhile... there IS no other week 22 pregnancy news. Which is why I've just spent this entire post rambling on about the position of my stupid legs. Join me next week for an in-depth discussion of how I brush my hair: because there HAS to be a wrong way to do that too, when you're pregnant, right?

Week 23
The Cold Cometh

So, I got the cold.

I always knew I'd get the cold – or possibly even the flu – at some point during this pregnancy (I mean, the odds of going a full nine months without so much as a sniffle must be pretty low, right?), and I even knew it would probably happen this week, too, on account of how this current variety of lurgy had already gone through most of my family, leaving me and Terry firmly in its sights. I was so worried about it, in fact, that I even messaged my midwife to ask her if I should just lock myself away now until the birth. (Answer: no, just wash your hands more often and don't be an idiot, Amber. Only in nicer wording than that, obviously...).

Since then, I've been careful to the point of paranoia about hygiene: washing my hands frequently, using hand sanitiser constantly, doing my best to avoid social kissing/hugging etc. (Full disclosure: that last one is mostly just because, GOD, I HATE social kissing. Please don't make me...) In fact, we've been visiting Terry's mum in hospital every day for weeks now (She finally got out last weekend, after almost four weeks: which is another story, for another day...), and my attempts to get through that hospital without touching any of the surfaces would be comical, if they hadn't been borderline *insane*. In other words, I've done absolutely everything in my power – short of literally just barricading myself in the house and refusing to leave, obviously – to avoid catching the cold, or anything else.

And I got it anyway.

Which actually makes barricading myself in the house seem like a pretty good idea, to be honest.

It started on Monday. Sore throat. Runny nose. The absolute conviction that, having somehow managed to keep this baby alive for 23 weeks, I was now about to kill it with the cold. Terry was assigned the task of typing variations on the words, "Will a head cold kill my baby?" into Google (I'm not allowed to symptom surf, and don't recommend that anyone with health anxiety ever consult Google on anything, because it will always, always give you the worst possible case scenario. Like, if you were to actually type that sentence ("Will a cold kill my unborn baby?") into Google, Google would say, "Yes, and it will also give you cancer!" Because, on Google, all searches eventually lead to cancer...), but no amount of reassurance from him that there was really no chance of my runny nose hurting my baby could calm me down. So I messaged the midwife again, to say, "You know that cold I was worried about catching? Well, I caught it! Will you just meet me at the hospital, or is all hope already lost?"

Or words to that effect.

Honestly, even in the midst of my panic, and even although the midwife has encouraged me to contact her any time at all, I felt like a prize idiot for doing it. I know it sounds spectacularly unlikely, but I'm actually not the kind of hypochondriac who runs to the doctor every time she sneezes. (Because the doctor would send me to the hospital, and in the hospital I would either die, or be diagnosed with cancer, obviously. Probs both.) No, really, I'm not. But I was so worried that my sore throat would kill my baby that I needed the extra reassurance. And then, when it came (Unsurprisingly, she just told me to keep my fluids up, and not to worry because my baby is well protected...), I totally didn't believe it, because how could I be feeling so bad, without it having any effect on a teeny-tiny baby that was totally relying on me? GAH.

Things I Have Worried About This Week:

As well as all of my stupid cold-related worries, I've been getting more and more scared about childbirth, and the prospect of being in hospital. Unfortunately, visiting Terry's mum in the place every day for almost four weeks has only increased my anxiety about it all, so I've been worrying about that, in between all of the other worrying I've been doing. Seriously, if 'Professional Worrier' was a legitimate career path, I'd be at the very top of my game right now, and probably earning a small fortune from after-dinner speaking and the like. I kinda wish there was a way to make that happen, actually.

As it happens, though, today, I'll be meeting with my consultant for the first time, to talk about my various fears, and see if she can help me figure a way through them. My midwife tells me this particular doctor is really lovely, and very understanding of mental health issues, so I'm not *too* worried about the meeting, although time will tell. And so will next week's pregnancy diary update – because I think I've complained enough for this week, don't you?

Reasons I Think I Might Want an Elective caesarean Section

1. I have yet to read a single account of natural childbirth that doesn't make it sound like a straight-up bloodbath.

2. A really, really painful straight-up bloodbath.

3. Which sometimes causes incontinence.

4. Rectal incontinence.

5. Oh, and vaginal tears. Need I say more?

6. The word "episiotomy" and all that it entails.

7. Labour. It doesn't sound much fun, does it?

8. The constant stress of not knowing what's going to happen, and when, if you decide to go with a natural birth. Sure, I know you can write a birth plan, but I also know that birth rarely seems to go according to plan, and what if my waters break in the middle of Tesco, say? And then I have to give birth in a taxi, and gnaw through the umbilical cord with my teeth? WHAT IF, though? Wouldn't it be much more civilised to just turn up at the hospital at a pre-arranged time, and have your baby without any drama, and without anyone having to gnaw any umbilical cords? Because I think so.

9. The thought that, if it all goes wrong, and I end up needing a c-section anyway, it could potentially require a general anaesthetic. And then I would die. Obviously.

And, I mean, OK, I'm being just a little bit facetious here. (And, again, I'm pretty sure that some of these fears are mostly informed by Neighbours, and other, equally implausible soap operas. But still.) I'm not exaggerating, though, when I say that the thought of natural childbirth absolutely terrifies me beyond belief. It always has. Because I'm a control freak: and control freaks rarely do well in situations which are outwith their control, do they?

This is why I have never understood the fixation some women have on natural childbirth, or the competitive need to prove how brave/strong they are by doing it all without pain relief. As I told my midwife at our first meeting, I want to have a baby, not a 'birth experience', and I want to have that baby in the safest, and least traumatic way possible.

I guess, as a c-section baby myself, I've never really got the stigma surrounding it: my own mum always talked about her own c-section in such a matter-of-fact way that I grew up accepting that c-sections were just one of the ways it was possible to give birth: maybe even a slightly more civilised way, if we're being honest. I still feel like that: which is just as well, really, because, given my age, I apparently have a higher-than-average risk of having to have one, anyway. Which is a problem, really, because the only thing that terrifies me more than natural childbirth is the possibility of having to have a general anaesthetic -which is how emergency c-sections are sometimes carried out.

So, in other words, if I decide to try for a natural birth, there's a good chance I'll end up with the worst of both worlds: all of the pain and fear of labour, followed by my worst fear of all - an emergency c-section, carried out under general anaesthetic. When you look at it that way, it's a bit of a no-brainer, really. And, as stupid as it might sound to want to have an elective caesarean section purely in order to avoid having to have an emergency one, I think that's what I want.
Now I just have to hope the doctor agrees.

Week 24
Decisions

Last week, on, "Amber Worries About Everything, OMG, When Will This Woman Calm Down?!" I had the cold, and was convinced it would kill my baby, even though every single person I spoke to about it – including my midwife – was all, "LOL, nope!"

This week, I do NOT have the cold! And no one died! And, actually, it wasn't even THAT bad a cold, now that I'm able to look back on it, with the clarity of a whole new week behind me. (And quite an important one, too: at 24 weeks, my baby is now technically viable, which means that if he were born now, he'd have a chance of surviving: wow!) As if that wasn't enough good news, however, the baby's movements have also been much stronger and more regular this week, which means I've had slightly fewer freak-outs than usual. I say "slightly" – I do still have my moments, of course, and, unfortunately for me, most of those moments seem to come right before my various medical appointments, which I'm pretty sure is the baby's way of trying to mess with me, somehow. Thanks, little guy!

This is how I came to find myself arriving at the hospital for my appointment last week, totally convinced that there was no point in even going ahead with it, because I hadn't felt the baby move in hours at that point, so some variety of Very Bad Thing had obviously happened: WOE. Luckily, there was a midwife present at the appointment (A real one, I mean: not a surly teenage one, like I sometimes get...) who was happy to doppler me then and there (I was well and truly doppled, my friends...), and, naturally, the second she put her hand on my bump, the baby kicked her hard, as if to prove that his mother is a lunatic – just in case that wasn't already obvious.

Which leads me neatly to the meeting itself, in which I carefully laid out my argument for an elective-c-section, and, rather than trying to talk me out of it, as I'd assumed she would, the doctor simply nodded and smiled, and said, "Sure! If you want a c-section, I'm happy to give you one. But just let me quickly go over some of the risks of it, first..."

And then she proceeded to scare me to death.

I went into the appointment convinced I wanted an elective c-section.

I left the appointment absolutely convinced that I cannot, under any circumstances, have a c-section: elective or otherwise.

Then I cried all the way home. So, yeah, I've been winning at life this week, for sure.

Reasons I Do Not Want to Have an Elective C-Section, Not Under Any Circumstances At All:

1. I could die.

2. The baby could die. And, OK, the chances of either of these things happening is apparently very small, but so were the chances of me having an ectopic pregnancy, or Terry needing a kidney transplant, and both of those things did, in fact, happen. When there is only a small chance of something happening, that still means there's a *chance*. *Someone* has to be the one to die in childbirth, after all: so why shouldn't it be me?

3. The baby could be cut during the surgery.

4. Or have breathing difficulties, which are apparently more common with c-section babies.

5. There's generally a longer recovery time.
6. And a longer hospital stay.

7. After the operation, I'd have an increased risk of DVT, which is one of my big health-anxiety fears (In fact, I'm pretty sure it was the thing that kicked it all off): I worry about it far more than is reasonable, and there's a part of my brain that's totally convinced I will one day be going about my business and just drop dead from a blood clot (I actually once had a colleague who this happened to: true story...), so the news that that day could be coming soon freaked me out pretty badly. What's more, I'd be wearing surgical stockings for the procedure, which is fine, but I'd also be sent home with a series of injections which I'd - get this - HAVE TO ADMINISTER MYSELF. Which, HAHA, NOPE. I mean, it's really cute that my doctor thinks I could give myself an injection, but there's absolutely zero chance of that happening: I'm actually NOT scared of needles when someone else is on the other end of them, but the thought of having to puncture my own skin makes me want to pass out with fear - as does the thought of basically being a ticking time-bomb, just waiting to drop dead. (Which, yes, is how health anxiety works. And also how DVT works, now I come to think of it...)

Conclusion: There is no possible way to get this baby out without one of us potentially dying in the process, so it's just going to have to stay in there forever. It'll be pretty inconvenient, really, especially when he's old enough to want to invite his friends round, and stuff, but it'll be less inconvenient than dropping dead from a blood clot, obviously, so I guess we'll just have to go with it. In the meantime, the doctor has arranged some counselling for me. I think I'm going to need it.

In less doom-mongery news, meanwhile, I'm pleased to report that this week we finally started to make some progress with my To Do list, and have begun emptying out the Room O' Doom (Formerly known as The Junk Room, but soon to be known as The Nursery...). While I'm still too anxious to risk tempting fate with any baby-related purchases, meanwhile, this week packages started arriving addressed to Terry (This was a big shock to the DHL delivery drivers, who are much more used to bringing me ASOS packages...).

It turns out that while I'm most looking forward to buying cute baby clothes, Terry's mostly been using this pregnancy as an excuse to accumulate gadgets. A video monitor. A breathing monitor. A room thermometer. Other things ending in the word 'monitor'. I know everyone will enjoy telling me that there is NO WAY a baby needs all that stuff, and that, in THEIR day they just stuffed the baby in a drawer, and that was that, but our baby, it seems, will have gadgets, and we're not sorry about it. (His mother, meanwhile, will have a new iPhone for her trouble. That has absolutely nothing to do with anything, by the way: I just want one.)

Oh, and when we were visiting my parents, who have been struggling under the weight of a baby-shopping ban (Things my dad has had to be talked out of buying so far: a ride-on car, a train set, a tiny Ralph Lauren jacket, and a small aircraft. And no, that isn't gender stereotyping, by the way: with the exception of the jacket and, well, the airplane, I had all of that stuff myself as a child, so he'd have wanted to buy exactly the same for a girl...), this weekend, I mentioned that Stuff had started to arrive, and my mum immediately left the room and returned a few minutes later clutching a packet of muslin squares. It seems that at some point in the last week or so, the strain of not shopping had broken her, and she'd gone rogue in the baby department somewhere. She had managed to restrict herself to just one set of muslins (Which she's now washed and ironed: awww!), but while I was writing this post, she's just messaged me from Sainsbury's to say she's bought some more, so we are sorted for muslins, people: I repeat, WE ARE SORTED FOR MUSLINS.

(We will definitely be needing more muslins, though.)

Honestly, I'm not totally convinced that there isn't a small, pedal-powered airplane lurking somewhere in my parents' house right now, but now that they know we've bought a few things ourselves, I guess it'll be a bit like that time the Chamber of Secrets was opened in Harry Potter, and who knows what will come out of it? Other than muslin clothes, obviously?

(There is still no sign of Shed Man, though. He has 11 days to make good on his promise to build the damn shed by the end of the month. Anyone want to place a bet on whether or not he'll do it?)

Things I Have Worried About This Week:

In addition to the whole, "how on earth am I going to get this baby out of me?" debate, I've also started pre-emptively worrying about post-partum hair loss. Yeah, I know it generally doesn't start until a few months after the baby is born, but hey, it's never too early to get in a good ol' worry session, is it? On second thoughts, don't answer that...

You know what else makes your hair fall out? Stressing over whether or not your hair will fall out. Pregnancy is just so unfair, really, isn't it? I mean, here was I thinking I was really looking forward to 2018, because I'll have my body back, and won't have to worry about medical stuff quite so much, but now I'm facing going into next summer bald, overweight (Because you NEVER lose the baby weight, apparently. Never.), and with my feet wrapped in a couple of old sacks, because none of my shoes will fit me any more, and I really can't afford to replace them all.

But it will ALL BE BE WORTH IT. Obviously.

Week 25
The Start of the Shopping

Alternative title for this post: "*I'm not crazy, I'm just a little unwell.*" Or, at least, that's the official verdict from the psychiatrists I saw at my first perinatal counseling appointment this week, anyway. (Er, she didn't actually say the last bit, TBH: that was Matchbox 20 who said that. Same thing, though...)

Because this was my very first appointment, it was more about gathering info/background information than anything else, so there wasn't really any counselling as such. I'm pleased to report, though, that not only did I not cry *at all* during the hour-long appointment (I mean, I came close a few times, and my voice did that weird, hoarse thing it does when I'm emotional. I call it my Man Voice.

Yes, it is just as sexy as you're imagining...), I also managed to cover everything I wanted to in regards to my precarious psychological state right now – and a bit more besides.

The upshot is that I'm going to be having one-to-one counselling, to try to help me get a handle on my anxiety, and she'll also be able to write some supporting evidence (along with the stuff my doctor and midwife will be submitting) for the hospital, in order to try to persuade them that it would be best for me if Terry was able to remain with me as much as possible during the birth etc. They're also doing their best to get me a side-room, as the whole "communal ward" thing has still been weighing on my mind (and Terry will definitely not be able to stay in a room with me plus five complete strangers): it's obviously not guaranteed, as emergencies are given first priority, for obvious reasons, but I'm hoping we'll be able to persuade them – mostly because I've spent the last couple of weeks looking into private maternity care, only to discover that, not only could I not afford it, I'd also have to travel to

London for it. Which wouldn't exactly be convenient, would it?Anyway, although I'll admit that I wasn't looking forward to this appointment, it was reassuring to be able to talk to someone who actually listened to me and took everything on board, without just offering up the usual platitudes, or making me feel like a freak for being so frightened of everything. She also told me that, actually, my fears are completely normal (especially for someone who's been through pregnancy loss), and that, well, I'm *not crazy*, basically. Other than that, though, if it wasn't for the bump and the kicks (Which, OK, are both pretty big things, to be fair...) I could easily forget I was pregnant most of the time right now – now those are words I never thought I'd type...

Things We Purchased This Week:

This week, after many long months of indulging my superstitious fear that if we bought a baby bath, say - or anything baby-related - the baby would instantly die, we decided to throw caution to the wind, and bought a baby bath. And also a bassinet, a cot, a changing table, and a cute little bath towel with bear ears.

So, preparations are well under way, in other words, and I'm not sure how I feel about that, really. I mean, we started making these purchases purely because the worry of not being prepared (Er,did I mention I'm a bit of a control freak? Yes, I am...) started to overshadow the worry of somehow tempting fate by ordering these things, but, I have to admit, I had a bit of a cry when the bath and bassinet arrived. They just looked so hopeful, somehow, sitting there in the kitchen, just waiting for a baby (Who will neither sleep nor be bathed in the kitchen, needless to say...) to fill them, and I know it's irrational, but as soon as they arrived, I was hit with this huge jolt of guilt, coupled with the unshakeable conviction that, if something goes wrong now, it'll be my fault for buying a towel with ears, and how could I have been so stupid, seriously?

Things My Parents Purchased:

Emboldened by her success with the muslin squares (Which have now doubled in quantity), this weekend my mum produced a small toy dog, (A cuddly toy, I mean, not, like, a poodle or something, although that would've been awesome...) whose name, she informs me, is Toby. She whisked Toby away again before I could get a good look at him, but he was very cute, so I'm sure I'll enjoy cuddling him when the time comes. I mean the BABY will enjoy cuddling him. The BABY. Ahem.

Shed Man Update:

I'm not even remotely surprised to tell you that there IS no Shed Man update this week – or, at least, there is still no shed, DAMMIT. This, our intrepid, shed-building friend (Note: not an *actual* friend...) informs us, is because his van has broken down, leaving him powerless to fulfil his promise to build us a shed. He even sent us a photo of the broken down van, surrounded by engine parts, and everything. It was quite artistic, in its own way, I guess: like, it would probably do quite well on Instagram-for-van-enthusiasts, if that's a thing? It's not helping me get my shed, though, which means we still haven't cleared out the cupboard under the stairs, and I'm very close to saying, "Screw this, let's just buy a new house that already HAS a shed!" Honestly, I'm starting to think that would be easier...

Things I Have Worried About This Week:

Finally, as I suspect will be the case from now until the end of this pregnancy, most of my fears this week have continued to revolve around two themes:

01. Is the baby moving enough?

And

02. How the hell will I get him out?

On the second point, I'm still leaning towards the c-section, if only because it will allow me to feel more in control of the whole process, but, at the same time, it will likely mean more time in hospital, and I can't even begin to describe how much that thought horrifies me.

Unfortunately, Terry's mum was re-admitted again this week (I've tried a few times now to write an update on this situation, but I just can't seem to find the words, so suffice it to say – for now, at least – that things have been very, very bad, but that when we visited today, she seemed much better than she has in a while, so we're really hoping she's turned another corner, and will be back out soon...): she's currently in a communal ward, and it just seems incredibly grim and isolating to me (We can only see her for a total of two hours per day, and there's a limit of two visitors per person), which, combined with the complete lack of privacy, at a time when she's at her lowest and most vulnerable, seems almost cruel, really.

Basically, the whole set-up, with the insistence on isolating people from their families, and taking away their privacy, seems horribly old-fashioned to me, and while I know it's something most people don't see as a big deal, I'm absolutely dreading it, so although the c-section seems like a calmer, more controlled option, the longer stay in hospital is a huge negative for me, as is the recovery time, obviously. One of the things I discussed with the psychiatrist was how, as a little girl, I used to get confused between the ideas of "hospital" and "prison". They both seemed more or less the same to me, except I knew people died in hospitals – and seemed more likely to get their own room in prison – so I knew which one *I'd* prefer, is all I'm saying. They still seem pretty similar to me now, to be honest, and the experiences Terry's mum has been having with our local hospital have only served to confirm my worst fears, unfortunately, so here's hoping the counselling will help with that.

Also, last weekend I randomly remembered the doctor telling me that there's a risk of them having to do a hysterectomy if things go wrong with a c-section and although the risk is a small one (and I think probably also applies to vaginal births) my brain has chosen to fixate on it this week, so... yeah, that's been a fun thought to fall asleep to, for sure. Why can't I just think about puppies, or kittens, say? Why do I always have to fall asleep to the image of me dying in a pool of blood? WHY? Honestly, right now both options absolutely terrify me, and I think it's going to take a bit more time to make a decision on this. Or a LOT more time, basically. Which is a bit of a worry, really, because I'm reliably informed that just keeping the baby in there forever isn't an option, which means I only have 15 weeks to decide. And counting.

Week 26
Half a year

It's been another one of those weeks where, every time someone's asked me how far along I am, I've had to stop for a few seconds and think about it, before going, "Oh yeah – 26 weeks!" Or six months, if you prefer, which is just... WOW. I've been pregnant now for half a year: it simultaneously feels much, much longer than that (When I think back to those first few weeks, it feels like a whole different lifetime), and a whole lot shorter, too. Similarly, I feel like the time remaining before he's finally here is both absolutely endless, and no time at all. Funny how that happens, isn't it?

So, week 26 has been a pretty hectic one: Terry's mum is still in hospital (Although doing much better than she was this time last week, thankfully), and Terry and I have both had a lot of work stuff to deal with, as well as all of the baby-planning. People tell such dire stories about life with a newborn, though, that I basically feel like once the baby is here, we're more or less going to just slip into a weird kind of coma state, which we won't emerge from for at least six months – or possibly not ever, if the worst of the stories are to be believed – so I've been doing my best to cram in as much as possible before that happens, including quickly polling all of my mum friends to ask if their feet changed size after pregnancy. Answer: no. There's always one, though, isn't there, and what are the odds that I will be that one? That bald, big-footed one?

Things My Parents Bought This Week:

1. More muslin squares.

2. Teeny-tiny socks.

3. A cloth thing which is apparently for swaddling.

4. A little pair of dungarees with an elephant on the front.

5. Fin, the Sheep Night Light. Who is a nightlight, but also a sheep!

Oh, and when I was speaking to my mum on the phone yesterday, I heard her say to my dad, "There's another bag in the car: it's the one with the pram blanket in it!" so either they've ALSO bought a pram blanket, or there's something else going on there that's just too weird to even think about. I'm guessing it's the pram blanket, though.

Things Amber and Terry Bought:

1. A tiny little Eames-inspired rocking chair. Because, this baby may not have a room to sleep in yet, but you better believe he has his own rocking chair. Priorities, people: priorities.

2. A very large quantity of wooden planks, to allow us to re-fit both the closet in the nursery and the linen cupboard. I'm actually quite excited about it, because, well, I have an entire Pinboard dedicated mostly to the interiors of closets, and I just can't wait to add my own to it. To move us further towards this goal, this week we sold the existing nursery closet doors on Gumtree (Because you can sell anything on Gumtree, seriously. I honestly wouldn't be surprised if one day Terry lists *me* there...): they were sliding mirrored doors, and I hated them with a fiery passion, so we're replacing them with non-sliding wooden ones, which will allow us better access to the space. When the people came to collect them, they all wished me "good luck" on the way out, and I'm honestly not sure if they meant, "good luck with the rest of the pregnancy," or just, "Good luck sorting out that absolute disaster of a room you've got there".

Apparently the room itself is one of those, "It has to get worse before it can get better," situations, though, and I honestly can't imagine how it could possibly get any worse, so I'm hoping that means we're almost there. Maybe.

Shed Man Update:

I just... I can't even, you guys. For reasons too complicated – and also dull – to go into here, the Shed Man basically owes us a shed at this point otherwise we'd definitely have gone elsewhere by now. As things stand, though, we're stuck with this particular Shed Man... which means we're stuck without a shed, as it turns out that building sheds isn't top of the Shed Man's priority list.

Terry is "handling it", apparently. I'm not allowed to "handle it," because, in an analogy that will only make sense to Game of Thrones fans, in this scenario (and pretty much every other scenario, really), Terry is Jon Snow, and I'm Daenerys. So, basically, he's all, "Look, guys, there must be a reasonable way to handle this," while I'm just like, "BRING ME MY DRAGONS, I WILL BURN ALL YOUR CITIES!" And I will, too. I can't, though, because, like I said, Terry's at the wheel with this one. He tells me he's "in daily contact" with Shed Man, and that he "has a contingency plan," but I'm not allowed to know what it is, because in the event that Shed Man fails to deliver on this, I will stop being Daenerys, and will basically BE the dragon. And no one wants that, do they?

Things I Have Worried About This Week:

Again, it'll come as no surprise to anyone to know that, the more time goes on, the more worried I get about the whole "pushing an entire person out of my body – or, alternatively, having him CUT out," scenario. It's ... not good, folks. Basically, over the past couple of weeks, I've become convinced – like, absolutely 100% convinced – that, no matter which option I go for, I'm going to die in childbirth. I am so sure about this that while half of me has been really enjoying the process of getting everything ready, the other half is just all, "I hope everyone enjoys using that sheep night light and all, because I sure won't be here to see it!" And I really, truly, think that, too: mostly around 20 minutes after I get into bed, at which point I start panicking about it all, and can't sleep. It's a bit of a bummer, really.

So: this week's diary entry started off with cute baby clothes and a sheep-that-is-also-a-light, and now it's ending with the literal fear of death: I think that's probably a good sign to wrap things up now, don't you?

Week 27
Sleep the Clock Around

Week 27 of this pregnancy has been a pretty significant one for me – for no other reason than that it's the final week of the 2nd trimester. In fact, by the time this post goes live, I'll be just embarking on the 3rd trimester, and, I mean, WOW, how trippy is *that*?

Speaking of Things That Are Trippy, how about this one: visible baby kicks! I've noticed my belly moving a few times lately, from particularly vigorous bouts of kicking, but this week I managed to capture it on video, so everyone else could see it, too. Not sure quite how much fun that video actually was for anyone else (although my mum watched it at least 1765 times, apparently), given that every time my belly moves from the kicking, I start shaking with laughter, which makes it look like King Kong is trying to break out of my abdomen, but hey, you have to get your kicks (Boom boom!) wherever you can these days, don't you?

This week I had yet another midwife appointment, and I think I have some kind of medical appointment or other every week now for the rest of the month. It's all a little bit overwhelming, really, given that my health anxiety normally makes me avoid any kind of medical situation like the plague, but it's all for the greater good, I guess, so I'm doing my best to just suck it up, like a good girl.

This particular appointment consisted of another blood draw, plus the anti-D injection I had to have at this stage, on account of my rhesus negative blood type, so I felt a bit pin-cushion-y afterwards. Still, the bump is measuring 28cm, so he's right on track, with a good, strong heartbeat, which makes me very happy indeed.

One thing that doesn't make me happy, meanwhile? Pregnancy

insomnia. Which leads to exhaustion. Actually, I'm not sure I wouldn't have had the exhaustion *anyway* at this point, because it seems like the kind of thing that would happen when you're lugging around a giant bump all the time, but the fact that I've been lying awake most nights, thinking about random crap ranging from whether I'll die in childbirth, to when I last saw that old towel that had been lurking in the linen closet before Terry emptied it out this week, hasn't helped either.

The tiredness hasn't been nearly as bad as the exhaustion of the first trimester, when I'd regularly fall asleep on the couch any time I tried to sit on it for more than ten minutes, but I'd happily sleep the clock around right now – which is just a little bit inconvenient, really, because I've been so busy with work, that I've had to just keep powering through it... and then lying awake at night, thinking about old towels. Because that makes TOTAL sense, brain, thanks!

Things My Parents Bought:

My parents are growing in confidence with their purchasing power every week now, so this week they brought...

1. A pram blanket.

2. A furry hat with ears.

3. A storage bench for the nursery.

Finally, this wasn't purchased by my parents, but here's a photo of me hugging a teddy bear:

(Also pictured: my bump. Not pictured: my face, because, damn girl, it looks like you've been storing up nuts for the winter in them cheeks right now...) Handsome chap, isn't he? This bear was actually a gift from Terry's mum a few years ago. I knew I wanted to pass him on to the baby, but he had the words, "GIFT COMPANY 2014" embroidered on one paw, which I thought might be a bit confusing, so my mum gave him a couple of new paw pads, and now he's ready to rock. Or whatever it is teddy bears do when we're not watching them.

Speaking of Terry's mum, she got out yesterday morning, after almost two weeks. This was her third hospital stay in the last few months, and it was a pretty bad one, but she's strong, and she's determined to meet this baby of ours, and while it absolutely breaks my heart to think that the likelihood of that happening is even in question, right now we're just glad to have her home, and are hoping to keep her there for as long as possible. Thankfully, the NHS have been pretty on the ball this time around, and have managed to arrange some extra help at home for her: she was already getting visits from the nursing service a few times a week, but they've stepped it up to two times a day, and there are plenty of friends and family members on hand to sit with her during the day, and stay the night if necessary. It's all unutterably hard, of course, and there's really nothing I can write here that will sum up just *how* hard it is, but, for now, she's over yet another hurdle, and that's good news, indeed.

As for Terry and I, meanwhile, there have been no major purchases this week, but Terry has been hard at work taking all of the junk that was in the "nursery, and re-distributing it around the house, where it's been joined by every power tool known to man, plus a really quite disturbing amount of cardboard packaging, which, where did it even come from?! The house is an absolute mess, in other words, and I don't just mean "by my standards," I mean, 'By *anyone's* standards." Seriously, who knew that clearing out two closets and one room would end up destroying an entire house? It totally has, though, and, at the time of writing, there are currently piles o' junk in every single room. Which brings me neatly to...

Shed Man Update:

So, after almost 6 months of swearing blind that he would *totally* be providing us with a shed, Shed Man has confirmed what I've been predicting since May, which is that, no, actually, he will not be providing us with a shed, like, what is he, a SHED MAN or something? I KNOW, SHOCKER, HUH?

Unfortunately, Terry's contingency plan (which, it turns out, was to buy another shed, which he'd seen on Gumtree) has also fallen through, which leaves us shed-less. And also speechless, to be totally honest: I'm trying very hard here not to use the words "I TOLD YOU SO," but, well, I *kind of just did*, didn't I? So, yeah, it looks like, on top of everything else, we now have to buy and build a shed. And if anyone's looking for a Shed Man in central Scotland, I have one I can definitely NOT recommend...

Week 28
Detour to Crazyville

So, week 28 has been kind of a rough-one, anxiety wise. I'm just going to get that out of the way up front, so that when this post takes a quick detour to Crazyville, you can't say I didn't warn you.

(The detour is coming up right now, btw. It's worth sticking around, though, because there are woolly mammoths later. Yes, really...)

See, health anxiety, as I'm sure I've mentioned before, is basically a form of OCD. People who suffer from it have, well, an *obsessive compulsion* to worry about certain things, or to constantly check symptoms. So, say someone who *doesn't* suffer from health anxiety/OCD notices their leg hurts when they move it in a certain way: they'll likely just think, "Ouch, that hurt a bit!" and go on with their day, won't they? The person *with* health anxiety, on the other hand, will repeatedly try to recreate that pain, by obsessively moving their leg around in the way they know will trigger it – not because they like pain, obviously, but in a futile, and ultimately doomed, attempt to reassure themselves that it's not happening any more.

(But, of course, it WILL still be happening. Because, like the fool you are, you've now *made* it happen so many times that even if your leg wasn't all that sore before, it sure will be now. Well done, you!)

For me, in the context of this pregnancy, my OCD has attached itself to a few different things, but this week – and I suspect for the rest of the pregnancy – it's been all about fetal movement. Yup, *that* again. The problem here, however, is that, unlike that sore leg (Er, I don't actually *have* a sore leg, by the way, although I think I'm *starting* to, now that I've mentioned it so many times...), the health service actually encourages pregnant women to obsess over the movements of their babies in the third trimester.

Well, OK, they don't tell you to *obsess*, exactly, but they may as well do: I've been given leaflets telling me I must make sure I monitor the baby's activity, and immediately report any changes; the pregnancy app I stupidly downloaded keeps encouraging me to actually count the number of kicks I feel every day, and, at every single appointment I have, I'm questioned about it, and reminded that I must be super-duper aware of every moment this baby makes. AS IF I WASN'T ALREADY.

Honestly, I suspect this would drive even someone without health anxiety to the brink of insanity (I have friends who've confirmed this to be the case), but given that I was standing on that brink anyway, is it any wonder that this week I fell right off, and spent many long hours lying on my side in the bedroom, drinking hot/cold/sugary/fizzy drinks, playing music to my belly, eating chocolate, and doing all of the other things everyone tells you will *definitely* make the baby move? Er, not really, no.

I should probably add here that I haven't been doing these things because the baby hasn't been moving. He *has* been. Sometimes in a way that makes it look like he's literally about to tear his way through my stomach, and emerge triumphant in the middle of the living room. So, honestly, there's been no real reason for me to obsess over this quite as much as I have – well, not other than the fact that I suffer from anxiety, obviously, and that this week? Anxiety has taken the wheel. It has made me feel like I can't really do anything at all, other than monitor those movements. Honestly, I've been reluctant to even leave the house, because how can I accurately count the baby's kicks when I'm distracted by other things? And, come to think of it, should I even be sleeping? I mean, what if this "change in movement" I'm supposed to be ever-vigilant about, happens in the middle of the night, and I miss it? WHAT THEN, PEOPLE?

So, it's been a rough ol' week, basically, made worse by the fact that this was Baby Loss Awareness Week here in the UK. Now, as someone who's suffered loss myself, I'm obviously well aware of the importance of this: in fact, I've written before about how I firmly believe that pregnancy loss should be talked about more openly, rather than swept under the carpet, the way it is now. As someone who's currently pregnant, though, I have to admit, I found it really, really distressing being bombarded by statistics about stillbirth etc every time I looked at social media. At one point, I was lying on my side, desperately trying to concentrate on feeling the baby move, when the news app on my phone flashed up an alert telling me that stillbirth is much more common than most people think it is – and, honestly, it just about destroyed me. I don't have news alerts switched on any more, needless to say.

That's the bad news. (And yes, I have a counselling appointment booked for next week...) There, was, however, also come good news this week, in the shape of my 28 week growth scan. Given that the baby had kicked me all morning leading up to it, and was still merrily kicking away as I sat shaking with nerves in the hospital waiting room, I was a little less nervous about this scan than I usually am, although, for me, that's still pretty freakin' nervous. Honestly, I absolutely hate these appointments, and, as I sat there waiting to be called in, I found myself really wishing I'd refused this one (It's not a scan the NHS routinely offer: I was given it because of my age, but the midwife had measured my bump and listened to the baby's heartbeat just a few days earlier, and had told me everything was right on track). Luckily, though, it all went smoothly: baby boy is measuring exactly as he should for 28 weeks, and is looking healthy, active, and almost exactly like Terry, which, WHOA. I swear to God, as soon as I glanced up at the monitor, I was just like, "Er, how the hell did Terry get in there?!" WEIRD. But also very cool, obviously.

Things My Parents Bought:

1. The entire contents of the baby section at Boots.

2. Things Terry and I Bought:
3. A pram. (Yes, I cried.)

4. Two woolly mammoths: one of which rocks when the baby sits on it, the other of which can be pulled along on a string. (Yes, I cried again...)

Finally, and in particularly earth-shattering news:

Shed Man Update:

Yes, I know, you thought you'd heard the last of this, but you are not so lucky, my friend, because THERE IS A NEW SHED MAN! I repeat: we have a NEW SHED MAN! This is NOT A DRILL!

So, after the absolute fiasco that was Shed Man 1, I'm pleased to announce that we're now about to embark on Shed Man 2: Return of the Shed Man, only with a new Shed Man in the principal role. I'm really, really hoping that New Shed Man is going to be the new and improved version (And, I mean, let's face it, he's not exactly up against stiff competition, is he?), and that he will, indeed, deliver on his promise to provide and construct a shed for us, on the agreed day - which is, just so you can all mark it in your calendars, October 27th. Now that we have the pram, and will shortly be taking delivery of a car seat, we really need to free up the space in the downstairs cupboard, and, being able to forget about this would also give us some time to concentrate on our next project, which has the working title, "How Can We Persuade That Guy Who Said He'd Fix Up the Car So We Can Sell It to Actually Follow Through on That?"

Or, alternatively, we could just call that one, "AAAAAAARRRRGHHHHH."

(I'm taking no part in this, obviously: everyone who comes by the house says, "Wow, I can't believe you want to sell that car – that'll be worth a bit of money one day!" And then I throw myself on the ground, and weep hot tears of misery, because, God, I love that car.)

And that was week 28, also known as the first week of the third trimester. It was messy, emotional, and contained a few more stray socks and historic meltdowns for my liking, but it also contained two woolly mammoths, a new pram, and, most importantly, the news that our baby boy is still doing well in there.

So it wasn't all bad, was it?

Week 29
No Guarantees

Well, it looks like we're doing this folks: I'm having an elective c-section.

(Or that's the plan, anyway: but more on that later...)

This week I had an appointment with my doctor, at which I signed the consent forms: which means that, at some point within the next few weeks, I'll get a letter in the mail giving me the date of my baby's birthday – how crazy is that? Although I think a planned c-section is probably going to be the best option for me, that doesn't mean that it's a particularly *attractive* option, though: I mean, all things considered, I'd ideally rather *not* have to be cut open on an operating table, you know?

Despite that, I'm going ahead, with the full support of my doctor and counsellor, for the simple reason that, with two terrifying options to choose from, this is the one that terrifies me the least – purely because it offers the least number of unknowns.

With an elective c-section, I'll be given a day and time to turn up at the hospital, at which point I know exactly what will happen to me. When I visited the labour ward, the nurse there walked me through – literally – the entire process, right down to showing me the room I'd most likely be waiting in before the surgery, and the route I'd take to the theatre. The word she used most often in describing the whole thing was "calm" – and that's a word I've seen come up again and again in the various stories I've read (and I've read a *lot*...) about elective c-sections. I like calm. Calm is good. And while I realise that vaginal births can *also* be calm, I think the complete uncertainty of what was about to happen would be really, really hard for me to deal with.

The deciding factor for me, however, was the realisation that, while there are obviously risks associated with c-sections – and I've gone through every single one of them in very great detail – there are risks associated with vaginal births, too. That's something the NHS *don't* always tell you.

When I had my first meeting to discuss the possibility of an elective c-section, I was given a long list of risks associated with the surgery, but absolutely none of the risks of vaginal birth. I had to research those myself, in order to compare the two: a task made significantly harder by the fact that the statistics on caesarean sections include *all* caesarean sections – so, emergency c-sections carried out under general anaesthetic, and with various complicating factors, are lumped in with elective c-sections, which are, broadly speaking, much less risky than those carried out as emergencies. The risks of vaginal birth, meanwhile, include tearing, haemorrhaging and incontinence, and many of those risks increase with age: so, for someone like myself, who's of what the NHS charmingly refer to as "advanced maternal age", and suffering from extreme levels of health anxiety/tokophobia, it's not necessarily true that a vaginal birth will *always* be the best or safest option.

It is, however, true to say that my age makes it more likely that I'd end up needing a c-section regardless of whether I want one or not. That being the case, and given my extreme phobia of general anaesthetic, I think I'd choose the planned c-section over the emergency one any day. So I did.

Of course, all of this could be purely academic. Although I'll be scheduled in for an elective c-section some time at the end of December (they're normally done a week before your due date), the baby himself obviously won't know that, so there's every chance that he could come early, and, if he does, that could end up being a whole different, er, birth game. If I were to go into labour naturally, I *could* still have a c-section, but it'll depend on a number of different factors, including what stage of pregnancy I'm at, and how quickly labour is progressing. If it were to happen very fast – which is unlikely for a first baby, but could still happen – and I rocked up at the hospital in advanced labour, I'd be advised to try for a vaginal birth, and I'm prepared to go along with that, given that the risks associated with a c-section at that stage would be higher.

So, although an elective c-section is my preference, I'm not going to insist on having one under *any* circumstances and I'm prepared for the possibility of it *not* happening, too. Ultimately, when it comes to childbirth, there are really no guarantees: which is something I'm going to have to spend the next few weeks coming to terms with.

In the meantime, though, there are a few things to reassure me: for one thing, my doctor has promised me that she will move heaven and earth to make sure that Terry is allowed to stay with me throughout the birth, and even afterwards, so I won't have to face my fears alone. For another, in order for that to happen, she's also going to do her best to make sure I'm allocated a private room in the hospital: again, there are no guarantees on this (In fact, if this pregnancy were to have a tagline, I think it would be, 'No guarantees'...), but the counsellor I've been seeing is also going to lend her support to this mission, which is a huge relief to me, because we'd probably have to sell our house to be able to afford a private room in the Lindo Wing, and it turns out that Terry isn't willing to consider that, just so I don't have to be around Other People after giving birth. Shame.

We may not have any guarantees, then, but we do at least have a *plan*: and that in itself makes me feel a little bit better about things...

Week 30
Pregnancy Hair

Some things I have had to stop myself Googling this week:

01. If I have to have a c-section with a spinal block, and I sneeze during it, what will happen?

Like, will my guts just all go flying across the room, and hit the surgical team in the face? Because it seems to me like that's EXACTLY what would happen?

02. If I have a c-section, can they just take my appendix out while they're in there? Also maybe my gallbladder, and anything else I don't really need, but which might start causing trouble at a later date?

Can you tell I've had a life-long fear of appendicitis? Mostly because, when I was a child, it was the only thing I'd heard of that I knew for sure would lead to me having to have surgery (See: phobia of general anaesthetic) and be in hospital (See: phobia of hospitals). (I also grew up terrified that I would get the consumption and die: thanks, Jane Eyre!)

(I am joking about asking them to remove my appendix, btw. OR AM I?)

03. "How to pee in a plastic tube"

If you're thinking this sounds self-explanatory, then I cordially invite you to go and try peeing in a plastic tube. Now I invite you to tie a beach ball to your stomach, and try again. Just for added fun, try doing this first thing in the morning, when you're so groggy you can barely even remember your own name, let alone why you're peeing in a tube. Not so confident now, are we? This graphic depiction of the third trimester brought to you by Forever Amber (TM): thanks for supporting the plastic tubes that make this pregnancy possible!

So, yeah, week 30. I kind of feel like I've crossed another one of those lines in the sand with this one: if I do end up having an elective c-section, it would be done at 39 weeks, and even if I don't, the consultant told me they'd be reluctant to let me go beyond my due date, so I really feel like I'm in the home stretch now. I mean, I technically could have this baby *next month*, people, and given that I already feel like I've been pregnant for roughly 1,000 years now (I expect it feels even longer for you, doesn't it? I am so sorry...), nine weeks really doesn't feel like that much longer, in the great scheme of things.

With that said, I'm pretty sure those 9 weeks will crawl by for Terry, my parents, and everyone else who has to deal with me right now, because I'm super-emotional over here, and liable to cry at the slightest thing. Pictures of baby animals are one of my biggest triggers, but this week I saw an old man out for a walk on his own, and it just about broke me. I mean, dude was probably just grabbing a few minutes of peace from his gigantic family or something, but I was fresh from a dramatic meltdown caused by Terry – get this – trying to film me on his Go Pro when I didn't know he was trying to film me – so my emotions are aaaaalll over the place. It is not fun, trust me. (Terry was filming me because he had the idea of making a little video for the baby – for when he's older, obviously – showing him some snippets of our lives while we were waiting for him, and how we were getting the house ready, etc. I think this is a lovely idea: my issue – and I'm prepared to concede that it was totally a hormone-driven one – was that, so far, all of the shots of Terry have been ones that he has planned and executed, and in which he appears as "fun dad", while all of the ones of me have shown me either in bed, with no makeup on, or looking down at my phone or something, with a furrowed brow and approximately 17 chins on display. Not. Fair.)
Also:

Snoring. GOD.

So, Terry informs me I've started snoring. "Like a pig," apparently. This has actually confused me, because Terry has *also* been snoring a lot recently, so now we each believe the other is keeping us awake with their snoring, and, well, we can't both be right, can we? Anyway, on Monday night my snoring was allegedly so bad that Terry had to go and sleep on the couch, just to get away from me. Unfortunately, he decided to wake me up to tell me he was doing this (Because he was worried I'd wake up, realise he was missing, and, I dunno, think he'd been kidnapped or something?), and he did this by standing at my side of the bed, kind of looming over me, like a character from a horror movie. I screamed the place down, then lay awake for the next five hours, so, yeah, no real need to sleep on the couch in future, Terry, just scare the crap out me and we'll take it from there, yeah?

The solution to this problem (And I use the word "solution" in its loosest possible sense, here...) has been for us both to wear nasal strips at night. I already wear my SYLA headband to prevent sleep lines, so between that and the nose strip, I have never been more glamorous, seriously. Or more tired, now I come to think of it.

In slightly less snore-worthy news, meanwhile...

I think I finally got the "pregnancy hair"!

I've been noticing for a while now that my hair *seemed* thicker, but over the last few weeks I've been finding much less hair on the floor after a blow-dry, too, so I'm thinking maybe this is IT, and that I'm finally getting to experience the thick, lustrous pregnancy hair I keep reading about, but which seemed determined to elude me.

I'm in two minds about this: on the one hand, I can't deny that I'm really enjoying the thicker hair, obviously. On the other hand, though, when I *didn't* get thicker hair, I thought maybe that meant I'd also avoid the dreaded post-partum hair loss, and, now that I'm not shedding, I'm guessing that won't be the case, and that, one day next year, I'll go into the shower, and emerge bald. I am quite upset about this: in fact, I know this sounds ridiculous, but I have literally – LITERALLY – been having nightmares in which I'm pulling giant chunks of hair out of the plughole, and the fact that this nightmare will likely soon be a reality is just... OMG.

Also, I kind of feel like I'm just being taunted with the thick hair now, and I'm preemptively annoyed that I'll only get to experience it for a few weeks, and then go bald and patchy. Hey, I wonder how much hair extensions cost?

Anyway, in the news that absolutely no one but me has been waiting for, I can now exclusively reveal that WE HAVE A SHED! Honestly, it's been a bit anti-climactic, really, in the way that only a garden shed can be, but the upshot is that I finally have my house back, and it's such a relief, I can't even tell you. (I'm going to, though...) Once he'd filled up the shed, and cleared the cupboard under the stairs, it was like Terry was suddenly hit with some manic kind of nesting instinct, so he's also cleared out the kitchen cupboards, his closet, and a bunch of other stuff I've spent the last few months nagging asking him about. I have never loved him more.

(My own nesting instinct kicked in about 5 months before I got pregnant, meanwhile, so I just got to sit there looking smug and going, "See, if you just tidied as you went, you wouldn't be having to do all of this now!" Yes, *I* hate me, too...)

Week 31
Very Tired, and Pretty Grumpy

This week I happened to overhear Terry on the phone to his brother, who'd presumably asked how I was doing. "She's very tired, and pretty grumpy, really," said Terry, "But I guess that's to be expected at this stage..."

"I AM **NOT** GRUMPY!" I yelled, grumpily. I stand by it, too. OK, maybe a *little* bit grumpy, actually, because, well, here are some things I'm really looking forward to being able to do again in January:

1. Lying on my back.

2. Lying on my front.

3. Rolling over in bed, without it feeling like a major production.

4. Being able to get in and out of bed without having to re-arrange a million pillows every time.

5. Painting my toenails.
6. SEEING my toenails.

7. Getting my eyelashes done – because these super-short eyelashes are making me look even more tired than I actually am, and apparently I'm not allowed to have either LV Lashes or extensions while I'm pregnant: boo!

8. Being able to eat and drink whatever I want, without having to meticulously check the labels, and then consult Google to find out if it's "allowed".

9. Running. Never thought I'd ever miss exercise (And yes, I'm totally aware that I could still go running if I really wanted to, I just can't convince my brain to actually do it...), but there's a growing number of things that I physically can't do any more, and I'm just really looking forward to getting back to something approximating "normal", and not having to worry about every move I make.

And, of course, I'm also looking forward to, you know, *having an actual baby* in January, although that goes without saying, doesn't it?

So the 3rd trimester is not a comfortable time, and this week I've really been feeling it. But let's move onto more positive things, shall we? Like the tour of the labour ward at the local hospital, which my doctor had arranged for me, in a bid to try to alleviate some of my hospital-related fears, but which I was secretly worried would just trigger even more of them.

As it turned out, though, this particular visit was actually really positive, and one of the best things I've done so far in terms of dealing with my anxiety. The midwife we spoke to was lovely, and made it clear to me that the hospital will do everything they can to help me through the birth process: I was really impressed with how clued-up they seem to be about anxiety, and how seriously they've been taking my concerns – honestly, I'm so used to just being dismissed (By the non-medical people in my life: everyone I've spoken to in the NHS has assured me it's totally normal to have concerns...), or told to not worry, because, "Everything will be fine!" that this actually came as a surprise to me, but they really helped to set my mind at ease a little. Don't get me wrong: I'm still absolutely terrified, and I know that's not just going to disappear overnight, but I do feel I'm getting a lot of support, and that's a big help to me right now.

The best part of this visit, though, came at the very end, when we were looking around the ward itself, and being shown the birthing rooms, etc. The labour ward has its own operating theatre, which we weren't able to see inside, as there was a c-section in progress at the time, but we were shown the room adjoining it, which is where babies are taken immediately after birth, to be weighed and checked over, before being returned to their mothers. Within seconds of us looking inside, the doors linking the room to the theatre opened, and two men in surgical gowns appeared, carrying the brand new baby that had literally just been born next door: it could only have been a few seconds old, and was still covered in fluid and screaming its tiny lungs out – we only got to see it for a couple of seconds, before we closed the doors, but Terry and I both got a bit emotional, and it was a nice reminder that, as scary as childbirth will obviously be for me, it'll be exciting too. If that's how emotional we got at the sight of a baby we don't even know, though, I can't imagine what we'll be like when we finally get to meet our own. Which will be happening in approximately 8 weeks, apparently. Gulp.

Week 32
A Date at the (Operating) Theatre

We have a date, people!

I actually wasn't expecting to be told this for another couple of weeks or so, but, early this week, I had an appointment with my midwife, who told me she'd just checked the system, and my elective c-section has been booked for...

December 29th!

This is, as you can probably imagine, is both really, really scary, and really, really exciting, in equal measures. On the one hand, I just can't wait to meet this baby, and the thought of having to wait another 6 whole weeks seems absolutely excruciating to me. On the other hand, though, my health anxiety now has Buddy Holly's 'That'll Be The Day (That I Die)' running through my head on a loop, and, in that context, December 29th seems terrifyingly close.

I mean, I haven't done even half of the things I wanted to do with my life. I never did get around to finishing the second draft of that book, for instance. I have yet to travel the world. And, to be honest, my sock drawer could be doing with a good clear-out, too. So much to do, so little time!

Still, all being well (and, obviously, the caveat to that is that I could technically go into labour at any time, so that date is far from set in stone), I at least have a set date to count down to, and that goes a long way towards helping me manage my anxiety: which is a good thing, because this week I had a meeting with an anaesthetist at the local hospital (Again, in a bid to try to alleviate some of my fears...) and it went a bit like this:

Her: So, why are you scared of general anaesthetics?

Me: Because they can kill you, can't they?

Her: Yes, actually, they can. I mean, not *all* the time, obviously, but sometimes they do, and the weird thing is that there's no way of knowing who they'll kill and who'll be just fine. So I understand where you're coming from, really.

Me: Er, so, given that they can kill you, I would ideally like to *not* be killed by one? If it's not too much trouble?

Her: Yeeeaaah. Can't guarantee that, I'm afraid. We'll TRY not to kill you, obviously, but I can't promise anything.

Me: It'll be fine, though, won't it? Because you'll do the c-section under a spinal block, rather than a general, yes?

Her: Can't guarantee that either, I'm afraid. Is there anything else I can help with?

Me: Could you maybe just kill me NOW, then?

And, I mean, those obviously weren't her exact words: they may as well have been, though, because there was so much, "Can't guarantee we won't kill you," mixed in with all of the more positive stuff that, once again, I cried all the way home. I'm making a bit of a habit of this, aren't I?

On the plus side, the anaesthetist DID reassure me that as I'm slim (I mean, God knows how she could tell at this point...), in good health, and haven't had any previous c-sections, I'm a good candidate for this procedure, which is *normally* straightforward. She also said that, while I can never eliminate the risks completely, a planned c-section will give me the *smallest* possible risk of having to be knocked unconscious (Everyone seems to be in general agreement that there's a good chance I'd end up needing a c-section even if I had chosen a vaginal birth), and that's one of the main reasons I'm doing this, so I guess that part was helpful.

I'm pretty much back to just wanting to keep the baby in there forever again, though. (Even though he just kicked me really hard in the bladder as I wrote that sentence...) As things stand, though, I have just seven weeks left in which to travel the world, write an award-winning novel, and, of course, clear out my sock drawer.

I think I'll probably start with the sock drawer, all things considered...

.

Week 33
Stephen Fry Can STFU

You know how, back in ye olden days, women who were about to give birth would basically just withdraw from society for a few weeks, and stay in bed, attended only by their ladies-in-waiting, or whatever? (Er, now that I actually write that down, I'm thinking it was maybe just *queens* that did this? Like, the "ladies-in-waiting" bit kind of gives it away, doesn't it? Oh whatever: I'm sure I saw it on The Tudors, so it HAS to be true, right?)

Who do I speak to about that, do you think? Because, the the fact is, I *really* want to retire from society for the rest of this pregnancy — and I think society would probably thank me for it, given that I am one grumpy biatch right now. Like, the next person to touch my belly while going, "OMG, it's HYYUUGGE!" *gets it*, not even joking.

Seriously, though: not only am I permanently exhausted, and not exactly bringing my A-game right now, I also suspect I'm not the greatest company, on account of the fact that the approaching birth, and everything that comes with it, has started to occupy my every waking thought. So, Terry will say something like, "Hey, did you see the news about that really important thing that happened this morning?" and I'll just be all, "BREAST PADS. I need to buy breast pads!"

Cute, Amber: real cute. Also, I apologise in advance to the friends who are coming round for dinner tomorrow, although luckily one of them is currently even *more* pregnant than I am, so I'm sure they'll understand if I start muttering about breast pads before falling asleep standing up or something.

Anyway, the big event of this week was what will hopefully be my final scan, which I had yesterday morning. This was just a routine growth scan, which I'm getting on account of my "advanced maternal age," and I'm happy to report that baby boy is measuring just fine: well, I mean, the sonographer actually said, "completely average," and I was a bit, "How dare you call my son "average?!" but no, average is totally fine by me.

Because I'm at a relatively late stage in the pregnancy now (I was 33 weeks 6 days when the scan was done), there's actually not much to see: the baby's head is so far down that I thought I was going to have to whip my jeans off at one point, to let the sonographer get a good look, and he's also big enough now that his head alone takes up the full screen of the ultrasound, so we didn't get a photo this time, or even a really good look at anything other than his little hands and feet ("He looks like a puppy lying on its back," was Terry's observation...), but they were very cute little hands and feet, so it's all good.

(Or, at least, I THINK it is: this particular sonographer was very quiet, and didn't really have much to say other than that she was happy with the measurements: which is exactly what we wanted to hear, obviously, but all of the other sonographers we've seen have talked us through everything they were doing/looking at, so I found the silence pretty unnerving, although it did give me ample time to consider the radiator hanging at ceiling level in the room we were in. Like, how did it get there? How do you change the temperature controls on it? So many questions...)

This week I also had another counselling appointment, and started doing some hypnobirthing. Honestly? I'm a little bit scared to admit it, because most people seem to present hypnobirthing as some kind of miracle cure for anxiety, but...I'm not really loving it. In fact, I am *hating* it: there, I said it. I don't know: Terry reckons I'm just too much of a cynic for this kind of thing to work for me, but I find all of the positive affirmations etc really cringey, and I've *always* found that *telling* myself I feel calm doesn't actually make me feel calm, so I think I'm failing at hypnobirthing, basically. Only me, right?

With that said, I also have to admit that I find it really, really hard to concentrate on stuff like this: I mean, I'm the girl who finds yoga really stressful - yes, YOGA - , purely because I struggle to stay focused on it, and end up thinking about whatever it is I was trying to stop myself worrying about in the first place. Yes, I know that means I'm yoga-ing wrong, but I can't help it: it's just so *boring*. Like, would it kill them to have the TV on in the corner or something? And why so *chanty*?

In other 'This is SO Me' news, I downloaded an app designed to help me drift off to sleep by having the dulcet tones of Stephen Fry tell me a long, and boring story, but found I was too polite to actually allow myself to sleep while he was talking, so instead I just lay there listening to a very long, very dull story about the lavender fields of Provence, and wishing Stephen Fry would just shut the hell up and let me sleep. I'm guessing this is one of the reasons 'mindfulness' doesn't really seem to work for me, then. I shouldn't be surprised, really: I mean, I must be the only woman alive who doesn't find bubble baths relaxing (Well, they're always either too hot or too cold, and, once I get them to the right temperature, all I can think about is how I'm going to have to clean the bath now, before I go to bed...), and I'm not too big on long walks, either, which are the other thing people always seem to be recommending as stress-busters. All that mud and rain, though: seriously, can I just... NOT?

Despite my hypnobirthing/mindfulness failure, though, I've actually been feeling pretty OK this week: yes, I'm still so uncomfortable at night (restless legs, mainly: a form of torture the likes of which I hadn't even imagined...) that I'm not really sleeping very well (Which is good preparation for what's to come, I guess, although every time I wake up at 5am and can't get back to sleep, all of those, "BETTER SLEEP WHILE YOU CAN!" comments start circling through my mind, and make me hate myself a little bit for being So! Wide! Awake!) but if being *uncomfortable* is the worst the 3rd trimester has to throw at me, I'll be very happy with that.
In other news, now that the nursery is finally finished, I spent a chunk of Sunday afternoon unpacking all of the baby clothes/blankets etc, and putting them into the closet and dresser:

(Yes, the **IKEA** drawer units are very securely attached to the wall, so no, he can't pull them down on top of himself, and, yes, I wish I had a pound for everyone who's helpfully informed me that he will 100% attempt to do this...)

I actually found this really emotional. Is there anything more hopeful - or, indeed, more heartbreaking - than rows of little baby clothes, purchased for a baby who isn't here yet, though? It's the feet. Those little dangling feet on the onesies, just hanging there, waiting for a tiny person to come along and fill them. I know it makes no sense, but those little feet break my heart on a daily basis: to the extent that, now that the nursery is complete, and the clothes are washed, ironed, and put away, I've had to close the door to the hall, so I don't catch sight of the room as I walk past it, and have to feel the weight of all the hope inside. I just keep imagining how it will feel if something goes wrong (And, for me, it's not really "if" - it's more like *when*...), and I have to come home from hospital and pack away that room: to take down all of the little dangling feet, and box up the blankets, and the toys, and all of the other symbols of a life that was only ever imagined.

Yes, I hate me too: don't worry.

I also know how utterly nuts I sound, by the way: I mean, even to me, the paragraph above sounds crazy in the extreme: I know that, but knowing it doesn't stop me feeling it, and it doesn't allow me to open the nursery door, or allow myself to believe that we haven't just made all of these preparations for absolutely nothing.

The worst of it is that, despite my deep conviction that there will be no baby to live in that room, or wear those clothes, my need to be organised means that I have no option but to proceed as if there will be. So, this week I re-packed my hospital bag, and filled the brand new changing bag with nappies and onesies, and other alien items that break my heart all over again, as I carefully fold them up, and put them into the bag, knowing that - if all goes well - when I pull them back out, it will be to dress my son in them.

I think packing a bag for a person who doesn't actually exist yet has to be one of the most surreal experiences of my life so far. He's yet to take his first breath, but he has clothes and toys, and a Jellycat bunny, who I tucked into the bag at the last minute, even though I can't possibly allow myself to even imagine the little hands who will hold it.

So I'm packed. *We* are packed. And the fact that I'm going to go into hospital as an *I*, and leave it as a *we*, is, without a doubt, the strangest thing of all.

Week 34
False Alarm

Welcome to Week 34 - otherwise known as, 'The Week Terry Freaked Out and Called the Maternity Ward in the Middle of the Night Because He Was Convinced I Was in Labour, But It Turned Out to Just Be Braxton Hicks, LOL.

So, yes, Braxton Hicks contractions: it turns out they're nothing like I thought they'd be. It also turns out that I've probably been having them for weeks now: it's just taken me this long to realise that the sudden hardening of the bump I've been noticing from time to time means there's actually something happening in there. Who knew?

Er, not me, apparently. I mean, I had obviously noticed that this was happening, but as it wasn't painful - or even particularly noticeable unless I happened to have my hands on my belly - I somehow didn't think it was worth mentioning to Terry, who's my usual sounding board (And chief Googler) for any unusual symptom. So it was only this week, when he put his hand on my belly himself, and then instantly recoiled in horror, saying, "Why does your belly feel like a rock right now?" that we realised what it was.

Once Terry had Googled enough to be satisfied that these were, indeed, just Braxton Hicks contractions, and not something to be worried about, we both went about our business as usual. That night, however, the Braxton Hicks started to get more frequent. Terry's in the habit of putting his hands on the bump last thing at night, when we get into bed (This is ostensibly to reassure me that everything is OK, but I think it's mostly to reassure *him* that the baby is actually moving...), and, that night, he noticed a pattern to the "contractions". (Which I feel the need to put in inverted commas, because, well, they're not *really* contractions, are they?)

"They're getting closer together!" he declared, consulting his phone, which he'd been using to time the tightening and relaxing of my bump. "They're down to every three minutes!"

"Better boil the kettle and thank God we've seen so many episodes of Call the Midwife that we'll know exactly what to do, then!" I quipped hilariously. OK, no, I didn't: and, to be totally honest, all I've really learned from childbirth scenes on TV is that it's possible to do it without removing any of your clothes. Or so it would seem, at least. (Also, until fairly recently, I assumed the whole, ''Boil the kettle!" thing was just so everyone could have a nice, fortifying cup of tea before getting stuck into the blood n' guts bit. The things you learn!)

(Oh, and AS IF I'd have allowed myself to watch *Call the Midwife* while I was pregnant. I've been scared to even watch *Neighbours* during the last 9 months, just in case they decided to run some kind of baby loss related storyline, that would basically destroy me, regardless of how unrealistic they decided to make it. Luckily for me, they just decided to go with the usual, 'Toadie's dead wife is back from the dead, oh no, wait, she isn't, it's just someone who looks exactly like her!"storyline. Phew!)

Wait: where was I? Oh yes: Terry was busy timing my Braxton Hicks contractions, and if you think I'm being weirdly dismissive of all of this, it's because I actually *was* weirdly dismissive of it all. It's very unlike me, I know - in fact, I think it's possibly the first time in the course of our entire relationship that I've been the 'sensible' one - but I just knew I wasn't in labour. For one thing, there was no pain whatsoever, and that didn't sound like labour to me, but for the main part, I just ... well, I just *knew*, really: not because I'm some kind of earth mother, who's totally in tune with her body, but because I'm such a hypochondriac that there's really not much chance of me somehow managing to miss any sign of being in labour: you can trust me on this.

Terry, however, *didn't* trust me on this... which is how he came to find himself on the phone to the maternity unit a short while later, while I paced around the room in agitation, worrying aloud if calling the hospital when it's not an emergency is possibly one of those things you can be prosecuted for, like dialing 999 because KFC are out of chicken, or whatever.

Answer: no, you do not get prosecuted for calling the maternity ward at 4am to ask them about your wife's Braxton Hicks contractions. It's not something I'd necessarily advocate, mind you, but, luckily for us, the nurse on duty was lovely: she reassured Terry that he'd done the right thing by calling them, but then told him that it sounded like everything was fine, so the best thing he could do for me would be to just let me sleep. Which, funnily enough, was more or less what I was thinking, too.

So, we went back to bed, where we reflected on the fact that we probably weren't going to get much sleep now, and then I lay awake for the rest of the night, worrying about how much our lives are about to change, and how totally unprepared I am for that.

The thing is, because I've been so focused on surviving the pregnancy itself, and worrying about the birth, I actually haven't really allowed myself to think about what life will be like afterwards (This is mostly a self-protection mechanism: I feel like I daren't let myself be too hopeful about it...), but this week it really started to hit me that I'm getting closer and closer to the end of this pregnancy, and that, all being well, I'll have an actual baby soon.

And, of course, I'm sure most women have the full 9 months to get used to this concept, but, like I said, it's only now that I'm allowing myself to even entertain the notion that it might all work out, and, honestly, it's pretty freaky to realise that, once this pregnancy is over, things aren't just going to revert back to normal again. I wouldn't say I was worried about it, exactly (People tend to be quite surprised when I say this, but it's true: almost all of my worries are centred around getting the baby here safely, and not dying in the process. To me, these are real, life-or-death kind of concerns, and I feel like, if I can get past them, I can deal with anything: so, while I'm sure it's going to be hard, it's – hopefully – not going to be *life-or-death hard*, and we have so much support from family and friends, that I'm sure we'll cope, however hard it gets...), but it's ... well, it's an adjustment, isn't it?

Speaking of adjustments, week 34 of pregnancy was also the week I finally cracked and started changing into my PJs right after dinner.

Now, I've never been a "PJs-in-the-house" kind of person, really. Which is not to say that I wear my PJs *out* of the house, obviously, it's just... you know how women are always going on about how, as soon as they come home from work or whatever, their bra comes off and the PJs go on? I've never understood that. In fact, to be totally honest, I've always wondered why they don't just buy a bra that fits them properly, because why would it be so uncomfortable that you'd need to rip it off as soon as you were through the door? Oh, the sweet innocence of ... well, of earlier this year, basically.

Well, this week I finally realised what that's all about, when it got to around 6pm and I was so uncomfortable in my clothes that I could have cried. (And they were all maternity clothes, too: I mean, it's not like I was trying to cram myself into stuff that obviously didn't fit.) The upshot is that I've bought myself some sleep bras, and am counting down to what my parents have dubbed 'Jammie Time' (STOP! JAMMIE TIME!) every night now. I also can't even fathom being any bigger than I currently am. It just doesn't seem possible to me, but then I look back at some of my early bump shots, and I remember thinking the same thing in all of them – even when I was, like, 12 weeks, or something, and just looked like I'd had a bowl of pasta for dinner.

If things continue this way, though, I won't be changing into my PJs after dinner: I just won't be getting out of them in the first place...

Week 35
Doesn't Time Fly When
You're Not Having Any Fun?

I think pretty much everyone I've encountered this week has commented on how quickly my pregnancy is "just flying by!"

Seriously, even the Hermes delivery man said it to me – although, to be fair, the Hermes delivery man is more or less part of our family now, we see him so often. (Totally not joking, btw – I've actually wondered if we should get the guy something for Christmas...)

Every time I get this comment, meanwhile, I just laugh hollowly and think, "LOL, NOPE." Honestly, I suspect pregnancy only ever really "flies by" for the people who *aren't* pregnant. At this point, though, I currently feel like I've been pregnant for at least 100 years – with twice as long still to go. I think these last few weeks are shaping up to be some of the longest of my life: I'm 36 weeks today, which is SO close to the end – especially given that my c-section has been booked for 39 weeks, so I know I won't go over that – but those three little weeks feel like an entire lifetime to me, and I've basically just resigned myself to being pregnant *forever*.

I know: dramatic, much?

On the plus side, though, time may have stopped moving forward – and I'm 98% sure it has – but, symptom-wise, week 35 has actually been not too bad, all things considered. For one thing, the baby moves so much (and feels so hyyyyugge) now that I haven't been having quite as many "OMG, I haven't felt him move in 30 seconds, WAH!" freak-outs as usual. I mean, I DO still have them, obviously – mostly in very public places, in fact, which makes me think the baby is just trolling me at this point- but, for the most part, he's big enough now that when he moves it sometimes feels like he's trying to fight his way out of my belly, which is as reassuring as it is occasionally uncomfortable. Seriously, what are you DOING in there, baby?

For another thing, although I'm feeling very, very large and clumsy, and walking up the stairs sometimes feels like an impossible task to me these days – like, can this girl get a medal or what? – for some reason I've actually been sleeping a little better this week, which is good, because, honestly, lying awake in those dark hours before dawn, and thinking about all of the things that could go wrong is NOT fun, let me tell you.

With that said, I may be sleeping *better,* but I'm still not sleeping *great,* and, as for Terry, I'm not sure he's been sleeping *at all*: not only has the poor soul come down with a bad cold this week, which he's manfully pretending not to have (Terry doesn't get 'Man Flu' – instead he just lies his face off and says he's feeling totally fine, even when he's blatantly not...), I'm also apparently snoring so much that at one point this week I woke up to find him huddled on the rug next to the bed with a pillow clamped over his head to try to block me out: whoops!

The irony of this situation, of course, is that Terry has ALSO been snoring lately – in fact, when I woke up that night, I was really confused, because I couldn't SEE him, but I could most definitely HEAR him. So, basically, we now have ourselves a situation whereby at least one of us is being kept awake by the other one's snoring every night: sometimes it's me, sometimes it's him, but either way, only one of us gets to sleep on any given nigh. So, yeah, that's fun, too.

This was also the week that our car seat arrived, and I bought an elephant. Well, adopted one, anyway: because the kind people at WWF (Er, the animal charity, not the wrestlers: that would just be weird...) sent me a little stuffed elephant for the baby, and when I read the accompanying leaflet, all about the declining number of elephants in the world, there was just no possible way I wasn't going to adopt one, was there?

Random week 35 pregnancy symptoms, then: dissolving into

floods of tears over the plight of the elephants. Wanting to adopt ALL the elephants. Also all of the dogs, cats, and random other animals that need it. Trying to convince Terry we need a micro pig. Being told that no, we cannot have a micro pig. Wanting to cry over this. Trying to convince Terry we should keep our old car, because cars have feeeeeeeelings too, and we cannot possibly hurt ours in this callous way by selling it. Being told NO. *Actually* crying over this. Being told that if I want to take over the monthly payments for the car, I can keep it. Realising I can't really afford it. Buying a lottery ticket instead, even though the website made me open an account and add £10 to it, and I'd literally JUST bought that elephant. I mean, *adopted* that elephant. Writing this long, stream of consciousness paragraph, even though I know I should stop now. Stopping now.)

And that was week 35 of pregnancy: it was a strange mix of elephants, car seats and lottery tickets, but I'm 100% sure I'm going to catch Terry's cold now, so I'm sure I'll look back on it with fondness when I'm lying in bed feeling like death warmed up soon.

Week 36
The Great Flood of 2017

This week brought bad news and... well, more bad news, basically.

The bad news is that, yes, I did, indeed catch Terry's cold: so *that* sucked.

The good news, however, is that that particular piece of bad news soon paled into insignificance when we somehow managed to flood the entire house.

Which was even worse news, really.

Now, when I say we flooded the *whole* house, I mean that literally: there's currently only two rooms in the entire house (living room and downstairs loo, just in case you were wondering...) which weren't affected by what we're thinking of as The Great Flood of 2017. This is to distinguish it from the floods of '14 and '08 respectively. It's... I mean, it's a long story, really. For now, though suffice it to say that we have form with this kind of thing, but that form didn't make it any less shocking when we woke up in the early hours of Thursday morning to find our en-suite bathroom filled with a pool of water, which was rapidly making its way across the bedroom floor, and down the stairs.

We still don't know whodunnit. We managed to establish fairly quickly that the reason for the flood was a running tap in the bathroom sink, but as neither of us has any recollection of entering the bathroom that night, let alone leaving a tap running in it, it's one of those mysteries that will probably get its own Crimewatch Documentary in a few years time, complete with a reconstruction, and a fresh plea for witnesses.

For now, though, all we know is this:

1. The tap was left running.

2. The sink doesn't drain properly.

3. The sink flooded the bathroom.

4. The bathroom flooded the bedroom.

5. The bedroom flooded the upstairs hall, and, finding it easier to seep through the ceiling, than go down the stairs, the water then proceeded to cascade dramatically through the light fixtures in the second floor hall.

6. It flooded the hall.

7. And damaged the ceilings of the office, nursery, main bathroom, and dressing room.

8. From there, it managed to seep through the hall floor, and pour down through the kitchen ceiling, onto the floor below, which we only finished installing a few months ago.

I don't recall how it happened, but we have obviously angered the Water Gods in some way, and now they have taken their revenge.

The good news is that the kitchen floor is fine: wet, but otherwise undamaged.

The bad news is... well, everything else, basically.

The bedroom floor is ruined: we had to pull it all up the next morning, and have already ordered a replacement, which still has to be installed.

The hall carpet, and ceilings of the various rooms, meanwhile, are all very, very water-damaged. The ceilings will have to be re-plastered and painted: the carpet really needs to be replaced, but there's only so much floor-replacing we can stomach in the space of a year, so we're just going to leave that for now, and just try not to look at it every time we walk along the hall.

Oh, and right in the midst of the drama, I realised I hadn't felt the baby kick in a while, and insisted on lying on my side in the bed for ten minutes, while Terry placed his hands on my belly in an attempt to reassure me that he could feel movement, and that the flood was going to be the only disaster of the night. (The baby was fine, by the way. Which is the main, thing, obviously, although the house being fine would *also* have been a good outcome to that particular night.)

The upshot of all of this, of course, is that this pregnancy is drawing to a close in more or less the same way it began: in a house like a building site, with no flooring in some of the rooms, and mess absolutely everywhere.

It's not really how I expected Week 36 of pregnancy to go down, really: and now, after all of our careful preparation, we have the added worry of, 'What if I go into labour and have to bring the baby home to a *literal* building site? I mean, is that even allowed?"

Thankfully, however, there doesn't seem to be a huge likelihood of that happening: my Braxton Hicks contractions are continuing, and, at my midwife appointment this week, I discovered that the baby's head is down, and partially engaged. Lovely Caroline was quick to assure me that none of that necessarily means that labour is imminent, though, so, to the surprise of everyone who knows, or has ever met me, I've been managing to stay relatively calm throughout all of this. Yes, I know: it surprised me, too.

And, I mean, I did have a full-on ugly cry when I realised the brand-new nursery had also been breached by the floodwaters, but, then again, I also cried when I saw an elderly couple holding hands as they walked down the street this week, so the pregnancy hormones are strong with this one, seriously.

Still, our new flooring arrived yesterday and will be being installed today, so hopefully by the end of the weekend my cold will have gone, the house will be looking like an actual home again (As opposed to just a dumping ground for DIY tools and random crap...), and I'll finally be able to relax a bit and ... I'm not going to say *enjoy*, because that would be a little too ambitious, but at least appreciate these last two weeks before we become a family of three.

Week 37
Ready or Not,
Here He Comes...

OK, so, now that we have the bedroom floor fixed, and the house back to normal, I think I can safely say – AGAIN – that, barring any further random acts of stupidity on our part, we are, once again, ready for this baby to make his appearance. Or as ready as we'll ever be, anyway.

This is good, because, as of today, I'm now 38 weeks pregnant, and this time next week – assuming I don't go into labour before then – I'll be at the hospital, being measured for a fetching pair of surgical stockings, and given some final checks before my c-section the next day.

GULP

Yeah, I'm terrified.

Like, ABSOLUTELY OUT-OF-MY-MIND terrified.

Unfortunately, I think the word 'TERRIFIED' (And note, not just "terrified", but ALL-CAPS TERRIFIED) pretty much sums up week 37 of the pregnancy for me. I really wish I could tell you that, once the house was back in order, I managed to totally relax and just enjoy these last few days as a family of two, but, well, you all know me better than that by now, don't you?

The truth is, almost as soon as the final plank went down on the new floor, my brain instantly switched from stressing over the state of the house, to stressing over the prospect of surgery. It's really all I can think about at this stage: well, that and how awful my life is about to be, obviously, because it seems the imminent end of the pregnancy has brought with it a dramatic increase in the number of people ready to tell me that I won't be able to cope, that I'm never going to sleep again, and to just generally assure me that if I thought pregnancy was tough, just wait until I try parenthood, LOL!

Earlier this week, for instance, I posted a photo of a haircut I was thinking of getting on Instagram Stories, and almost immediately got a flurry of messages urging me to THINK ABOUT THE BABY and warning me that I just won't be able to handle a haircut *and* a baby. Like, no one has ever been able to do that, apparently.

Now, this was a really simple haircut we're talking about: it's one I've had before a few times now and it seriously isn't any more maintenance than my hair is now. NOPE, though: from what I'm told, this cut would be way, way too ambitious for me, and I can either have very slightly different hair *or* a baby, but definitely not both, because that's just crazy talk, isn't it?

So, this kind of thing is pretty daunting to read, really, because while the comments were, ostensibly, about hair, the message is pretty clear, and the message I took from it all, was, "Amber, you are not going to cope with this. Seriously, you're not even going to be able to style your hair in a couple of weeks time, because *that's* how tired you're going to be, and *that's* how much you're going to struggle."

Which...yeah. Add to this, all of the "better sleep now!" and "JUST YOU WAIT!" comments, and, to be honest, I almost feel like people are setting me up to fail, you know? I can't help but wonder how much of all of this becomes a self-fulfilling prophecy, too: I mean, if people keep on telling me I'm not going to be able to cope, and I therefore go into it with that expectation, then will that make it harder for me to cope? Because, right now, all of the doom-mongering has made me feel like Terry and I are about to disappear into some kind of black hole for the next few months, during which we will be basically unable to function, or do even the simplest of things. I've tried my best to plan ahead as much as possible for this, but I have to admit, I'm pretty damn scared by it, and have had more than a couple of moments this week where I've read yet another, "Your body will never be the same again!" or "You just don't know what exhaustion really is, but you will soon!" comment, and have genuinely wondered what the hell I've let myself in for.

Of course, there's really not much I can say to any of this. I mean, it's not like I can change my mind now, or decide not to go ahead with the birth: one way or another, this baby is going to have to get out of there, so I'm doing my best to ignore the doom-laden comments and just try to focus on getting through this surreal, limbo-like time before the birth, day by day. One of those days will be Christmas, obviously, which is both a blessing and a curse: it's a blessing in that it will, at least, provide a bit of a distraction, but honestly, I'm so focused on next Friday (and everything that will come after it) that I can't bring myself to even think about Christmas right now. Or, you know, anything other than the fact that, this time next week, I'll be less than 24 hours away from meeting my baby boy for the first time.

I'm excited about that obviously – hopefully that goes without saying – but, of course, pregnancy after loss, or when you're dealing with severe anxiety, plus a generous dose of hospital phobia, is a pretty hard thing to get through, and, in my case, I think the only way I've been able to get to this stage has been by living in a kind of denial that "this stage" would ever come, and, now that it has, it's made everything feel incredibly surreal. I just can't seem to get my head around the fact that I'm actually going to have a baby next week – and I'm still too scared to be able to trust that it'll actually happen, without something going catastrophically wrong.

Unfortunately for me, my brain has no shortage of catastrophic scenarios it's willing to present me with, so while week 37 hasn't really been any different from week 36 in terms of symptoms etc, it has been a challenging one mentally – and I don't think week 38 is going to be any easier, really.

Still, one thing I know for sure, is that week 38 – however it pans out – will definitely be the last week of this pregnancy, which is just... WOW. I feel like I should have something profound and moving to say about this, but, honestly, at this point it's a miracle that I can still express myself at all, let alone say something even remotely eloquent. Instead, then, I'll just say this:

8 MORE DAYS TO GO.

(Oh, and yes, I DID get the haircut – or a version of it, anyway: pray for me...)

My C-Section Birth Story

Max Miaoulis was born at 11:51am on a snowy December morning, at the very end of the year.

The previous day, I'd gone into hospital for my "clerking" appointment: they'd taken blood, measured me for the surgical stockings I'd have to wear during and after the operation, and given me a small package of pre-op meds: one antacid pill to take at 10pm that night, and another which I was instructed to take at 6am the next morning, along with two energy drinks.

I was also told to fast (other than water) from 2am onwards, and to not even have water after I'd taken my meds on the morning of the surgery. Everyone I encountered at the hospital over the next two days made a huge deal about how hungry I was going to be, but honestly, I already felt so sick with nerves that I had my doubts about how I was even going to manage to choke down those two drinks. (Also, my surgery was scheduled for 9am, and not eating between 2am and 9am isn't really "fasting" as far as I'm concerned: it's just "night-time"...)

Everything already felt totally surreal to me by this point. It so happened that my friend Mhairi had had a baby the day before, in the same hospital: she and her husband were getting ready to leave just as we arrived, so we managed to duck out of our appointment and go and meet them in the hospital corridor, to quickly say hello to the new baby, who was absolutely gorgeous.

"Can you believe we're going to have one of those by this time tomorrow?" I asked Terry, as we walked back to the ward. No, Terry could not believe it: and I DEFINITELY couldn't - in fact, I was so sure something was going to go catastrophically wrong

(Context: tokophobia) that, while I'd stopped short of making a will, I had left him with a bunch of instructions for my untimely demise. Stuff like, "Burn my diaries without reading them," and, "Play Heaven Knows I'm Miserable Now at the funeral," - that kind of thing. Well, you can't be too well prepared, can you?

Anyway! The rest of the day passed in a complete, "I'm having a baby tomorrow" blur. We visited Terry's mum, then had a visit from my parents (I was obviously assuming that this was the last time I would ever see all of these people, so I was a complete emotional wreck...). I decided I'd like a bacon roll, as a kind of, "The condemned woman ate a hearty meal," kind of thing, but the shop we stopped at had sold out, so that was just BRILLIANT, obviously, and TOTALLY a sign that everything was going to go wrong, I mean, OBVIOUSLY, right?

(Yeah, complete wreck. Also, oh hey, look, I'm 769 words into this, and I've still not even got to the day of the birth! Could someone please hand me a grip, here?)

Anyway, back at home I had a huge plate of pasta for dinner, plus a baked potato (I'd been instructed to have lots of carbs, and I was happy to comply with that...) and Terry and I spent our last night as a family of two binge-watching This Is Us (Which is awesome, seriously. Like, I don't know why you're reading this rambling blog post, when you could be watching it, instead?), before heading to bed at around 11pm.

I really didn't think I'd sleep much that night, but sometimes when I'm facing something really, really scary, I enter a strangely calm stage right before it, so I actually did get a few hours sleep, before waking up at around 5am, an hour before my alarm. I lay in bed for a while, mulling over the thought that this was the day I was going to have a baby and/or die, until it was time to get up and take the rest of my meds.

The two drinks tasted like very cheap candy, and I only made it through one and a half bottles before my churning stomach forced me to stop. Then I had a quick shower, got dressed in my trusty maternity leggings and top, and it was time to go.

OMFG.

I can clearly remember walking downstairs, thinking with every single step that the next time I did this, I'd have a baby (Or I'd be dead, and this would be the LAST! TIME! EVER! that I'd walk down the stairs in my house: woe! Drama!). I had a brief freak out in the kitchen doorway, when I burst into tears and told Terry that, actually, you know what, I absolutely, positively could not - and WOULD not - do this, but he gently prised my fingers off the door jamb, and steered me out to the car. (Last time I'd ever get into a car! Last time I'd ever buckle a seat belt! The drama is STRONG in this one, folks...)

It was still pitch dark outside, and had snowed overnight, which made the drive to the hospital feel every bit as surreal as everything else at that point. Once there, we parked outside Labour & Delivery, unloaded my three hospital bags (Two for me, one for the baby. I barely even opened any of them...), and headed inside. "Big day today, then!" said a woman we passed in the corridor, nodding at our collection of bags. I only managed a weak smile in response, but at least I managed to refrain from saying, "YES, I'M HERE TO DIE!" which is what I was thinking, so at least that's something.

We headed upstairs to the maternity ward, which was in complete darkness, with a bunch of nurses milling around looking confused. "We're not quite ready for you yet," one of them told us, before showing us into a waiting room, which had obviously been used for Christmas dinner: there was a long trestle table with a Christmas-themed cloth on it, a tree blinking away in the corner, and a general air of, "I'm trying to be festive, because it was Christmas this week, but, actually, I'm a hospital waiting room, so ain't nothing I can do to be even remotely 'festive', no matter how many Christmas baubles you throw at me: sorry!"

I'd been told there were three c-sections scheduled for that morning, and, sure enough, we were soon joined by two other couples, all looking every bit as nervous as I felt, although significantly more glamorous. Like, one of the other women was in full makeup, with her hair styled, and a set of long false nails, which had presumably been freshly applied for the occasion. And there was me: white faced, terrified, and just that second realising that I hadn't even combed my hair before leaving the house.

"No one has nearly as many bags as you!" hissed Terry, who had taken issue with my over-packing.

"No one needs as much makeup as me!" I replied - which was a truth I felt should be self-evident, given that I was sitting there looking like Casper the Friendly Ghost. GOD.

So, we waited.

Then we waited some more.

We waited so long, in fact, that it became painfully obvious that I would not be having my surgery at 9am - which was unfortunate because I knew that the longer I had to wait, the more nervous I'd get. I'd been promised I'd be first in the queue, (Assuming there were no emergencies that day, which would obviously take priority) for this very reason, but the hospital staff had seemed almost surprised to see us, which made me wonder what else would go wrong.

"It'll be the private room," I told Terry, grimly. "What do you want to bet they don't have a private room?"

Because of my tokophobia/fear of hospitals, my doctor had very kindly arranged for Terry to be allowed to stay overnight in the hospital with me - which was obviously going to necessitate me being given a side room. (In Scotland, partners are not normally allowed to stay overnight, and you can't pay for a room or book one in advance, unfortunately, otherwise I'd happily have done that.) I'd been promised over and over again that this fact was all over my notes, and that the staff on the ward would know all about it - so, obviously I was totally convinced that, no, they wouldn't, and that they wouldn't have a side room for me.

They did not have a side room for me.

Or, rather, they DID - but they refused to give it to me, saying that, as I was having a c-section, I'd have to be on a communal ward, so they could keep a closer eye on me. No, the promise of a side room was not recorded in my notes, I was told, so, instead, I was shown to a bed in a crowded ward, with barely any room between it and the next bed, and definitely no room for Terry to stay overnight.

Yeah, I cried.

I'm embarrassed to admit it, because I realise it makes me sound like an absolute princess, but I'd had months of counselling to try to help me deal with my fear of the hospital, and the only thing that had *actually* helped me was the promise that I'd be given a private room. I was absolutely horrified by the thought of having to be on a communal ward after the surgery, when I knew I'd be at my most anxious, and I had no idea how I'd cope on my own with a new baby, when I presumably wouldn't even be able to get out of bed.

So, yeah, it was not my finest hour - and it got worse when I was handed a package consisting of two surgical gowns, a pair of white knee socks, and a cardboard box, and instructed to change into the clothes in the ward's shared toilet, and - oh yeah, if I could just pee in that box, too, that would be grand.

I did as instructed, leaving Terry to try and argue my case with the head nurse - who was clearly not for budging. Thankfully, though, by the time I emerged, wearing one surgical gown on my front, and another on my back, like a cape, Terry had persuaded her to call my doctor, who'd been all, "For the love of God, give this woman a side room, like we arranged weeks ago!" (When I saw her the next day, she told me she'd wanted to beat her head against the desk when they told her they were trying to put me on a ward...) and I was finally shown into a room.

I had never looked sexier:

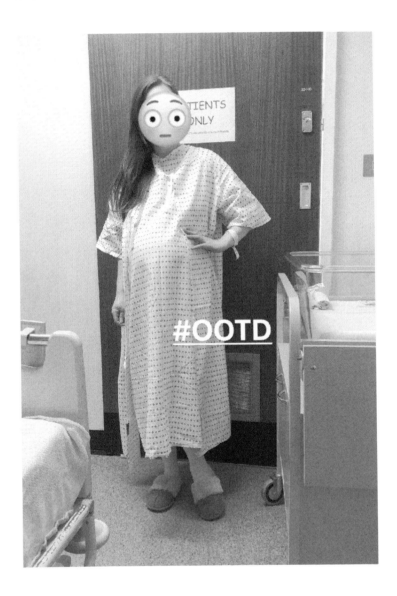

(Excuse the emoji - my face was so swollen by this point that I almost burst into tears when I saw this photo...)

At this point, I was introduced to Katie, who'd be my midwife while I was on the ward. (And who confirmed that she'd seen my notes, and that yes, the instructions about Terry staying with me were, indeed, all over them...) She was absolutely lovely, and really made me feel like I was in safe hands, so I started to calm down just a little bit. By this stage, though, it was well past 9am, and Katie told me one of the other women had been taken down to theatre before me (I think there had been some concern about her baby when they'd done the ante-natal check, so she'd been taken as an emergency), so my surgery had been pushed back. While we waited, Katie did a final check on the baby, and we heard his heartbeat for the last time (This made me really emotional: I just couldn't believe we were actually about to meet him, after all this time...), before sitting down to wait. And wait. And wait.

And take photos of the sign on the bathroom door:

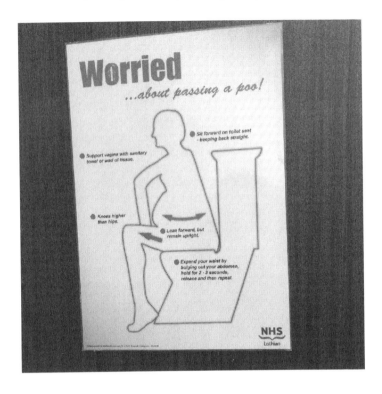

It's the choice of an exclamation mark rather than a question mark that intrigues me here. It's not, "Worried about passing a poo?" it's, "Worried about passing a poo!" Which is an oddly jaunty way to phrase this particular issue, don't you think?

Seeing as we've already taken this detour into Too Much Information, I'll just quickly add that I wasn't worried about "passing a poo"... until I saw this sign on the bathroom door. And then it was pretty much all I could think about.

I took this opportunity to message my parents, who I knew would be almost as anxious as I was at this stage, and then Terry and I sat side by side on the bed, watching the snow fall outside the window, and trying to come to terms with the fact that we were about to become parents really, *really* soon.

I never did come to terms with this, by the way. I was still 100% convinced that one or both of us - me and the baby, I mean, not me and Terry - was going to die...

I'd been worried about the effect any delay in proceedings would have on my mental health, but, as it turned out, the time passed really quickly (Mostly due to the 345,875 trips I made to the bathroom...), and before long, Katie was back, this time with a hospital porter, who, she said, would be taking my bed down to the labour suite. This totally confused me - like, who were they giving my bed to, and where would I sleep after the operation? - until Terry told me they were taking it there so that I could be put into it after the surgery. Which was, it seemed, imminent.

Sure enough, a few minutes later, Katie was back.

"Are you ready to do this, then?" she asked, smiling. And honestly, I considered saying "no". That didn't really seem to be an option, though, so, instead I followed her out of the room, and she, Terry and I walked down to the Labour Suite. At this point, I finally got the answer to one of my many hospital-related questions: would I have to walk through the public part of the hospital in my surgical gown and socks, or was there, perhaps, a network of secret passages for this kind of thing, a bit like in the Magic Kingdom?

Folks, it was NOT like the Magic Kingdom.

Like, not even a little bit.

Nope, I did a walk of shame - I will refer you at this point to the photo above - through what felt like many miles of hospital corridors, plus a ride in one of the lifts. I'd ordinarily have been mortified by this, but hey! I was on my way to ~~certain death~~ have a baby, so bad fashion was the least of my worries, really.

(On a related note, I think I know exactly how Anne Boleyn must have felt as she walked to her execution. She was probably a *bit* better dressed than me, though...)

Once in the labour ward, we were shown into the room I'd visited a few weeks earlier during my tour of the ward, and Katie handed me over to another midwife, who'd be looking after me during the procedure. I really wish I'd paid more attention to this woman's name, because she was absolutely fantastic, but I could barely remember my *own* name at this point, so... yeah. Anyway, the midwife gave Terry a set of scrubs to change into, so he could finally live out his dream and pretend to be a real doctor, and then the anaesthetist arrived to put the fear of God into me. Or, at least, I'm assuming that was the purpose of her visit: it was certainly the consequence of it, anyway.

I'd actually requested - and been promised - that I not be taken through the risks of the procedure yet again, because I knew it wouldn't be helpful at that stage, but, yeah, she totally went through all of the risks of the procedure again, and, yeah, as soon as she left the room, I burst into tears and told Terry I wasn't going to be able to go through with it, so could he just take me home now, yes?

(NO.)

"Yes, you could die during this procedure," said the anaesthetist cheerfully, as she left the room, "But you could also die in a car crash on the way home from the hospital, couldn't you?"

So that was helpful.

A few minutes later, though, the surgeon appeared to talk to me. I'd hoped my regular doctor would be performing the surgery, but she was working in another hospital that day, so instead I got Maeve, who was absolutely lovely, and who managed to talk me down from the mental ledge I was on. She asked at this point if I wanted her to talk me through the procedure as she was doing it, but my answer to that was a firm NO. I was just all, "Do what you have you do, but don't tell me what that is." I mean, I was pretty clear that she was going to cut me open and extract a baby: what more did I need to know, really?

Finally, it was GO time.
I walked into the theatre, which was weird in itself: most people don't actually see the inside of an operating theatre, as they're normally unconscious by that point, but I was very much awake, and had to make an effort not to look around too much - I didn't want to see any of the surgical equipment that was about to be used on me, and I particularly didn't want to have to see the little incubator waiting hopefully at the side of the room for the baby who was about to be born.

The room was really cold, and seemed to be filled with people. I'd been warned in advance that there would be a lot of people present, but I was still a bit surprised by it, although I guess it was reassuring in a way to know there were plenty of people there to keep an eye on me, and to shout, "We're losing her! Give me 20mls of epinephrine, STAT!" when necessary.

As soon as we got into the room, I was taken over to the operating table (This was actually my first surprise, as it was a narrow bench, not the large dining table affair I'd been imagining...), and divested of my underwear, plus one of my two surgical gowns, before being helped up to sit sideways on the table. At this point I was painfully aware that I was flashing my bare butt to a room full of people, but honestly, by that point they could have paraded everyone I've ever met through that room, and I don't think I'd have cared. Because it turns out that the prospect of being imminently cut open has a way of really focusing the mind, you know?

At this point, I was given a pillow to hold, and instructed to kind of crouch over it, so my back was as steady as possible. I'd already been talked through exactly what would happen during the surgery, so I'd expected this part, but not the next bit, where my back was sprayed with freezing cold mist (Some kind of antiseptic, I think), and a plastic sheet was stuck onto it. (Another one of these was later attached to my torso, apparently, although I knew nothing about that one. As it turned out, I had some kind of allergic reaction to the adhesive they used on these, and was horribly itchy for around 24 hours after the operation, with an attractive rash on my torso and back: up until then, I'd always answered "no" to the "any allergies?" question you're asked constantly when you're pregnant, so it figures my very first allergy would turn out to be something surgery-related...)

Terry was shown to a seat right in front of me (Partners aren't normally brought into theatre until the spinal block is in place, but the hospital had made an exception for us, in the belief that he would help keep me calm. Well, he did his absolute best, bless him, but he looked so terrified all the way through it that I felt like I should be comforting him instead...), and everyone seemed to crowd around me while the anaesthetist examined my back, ready to administer the spinal block. While this was happening, someone else was putting a venflon into the back of my hand (Everyone told me this would be the most painful part of the procedure, but I honestly don't remember anything about it...), and attaching various monitors and tubes to me, and it all got a bit much, at which point I burst into tears: #GIRLBOSS.

Luckily, my midwife was absolutely fantastic, as I said. Her job was to basically keep an eye on me during the surgery, and make sure I was as happy/comfortable as possible. As soon as she saw that I was getting distressed, she made everyone take a step back, and give me a few minutes to calm down. I was really embarrassed, particularly given that I didn't really know why I was crying (Or not exactly, anyway: I mean, I knew I was so paralysed with fear that they probably wouldn't need the spinal block, but I didn't know why the tears came at that exact moment...), but everyone was so kind, and gave me a moment to get a grip, before they got back to work.

First of all, the anaesthetist injected local anaesthetic into my back: it was sore, yes, but no more so than any other injection/blood draw, really. It obviously worked, too, because I didn't feel the spinal go in AT ALL: I just knew it was done because - and this is weird - my butt started to feel hot, quickly followed by my legs, which got warm and tingly from the toes up: such a weird feeling!

As soon as the tingling started, I was moved onto my back. Unfortunately for me, I didn't realise that the bench I was on was designed to tilt to the side, so I thought I was about to roll off it, and let out one of my patented Silly Girl Squeals, which made everyone laugh. So, yeah, I was acquitting myself MARVELLOUSLY at this point, I really was...

So, they put me on my back, and started to put up the screen that would stop me seeing what was going on once the surgery got started. My next surprise was the fact that the "screen" was partly just my own hospital gown, hooked up in front of me, at chest level: as they pulled it up, I noticed that it was spattered with blood, and had a horrible moment when I thought I was wearing someone else's dirty gown, before Terry - who was seated at my head - told me the blood was from the spinal: whoops!

By now, my legs were feeling seriously tingly. The anaesthetist asked me to raise them off the table, and I was absurdly disappointed when I only managed to lift them a couple of inches (My ab muscles have never been that great though, tbh...) - which was obviously stupid of me because that was *kind of the whole point, Amber*, D'UH. In all of my anticipation of the c-section, though, I'd totally failed to consider how my health anxiety would play out in theatre, and, when it came down to it, I actually found it quite frightening to be paralysed from the chest down, and unable to feel/move my legs - in fact, I had to work really hard to fight the impulse to try to wiggle my toes all the time, just to see if I could. I even did a panicked, "I CAN'T FEEL MY LEGS!" speech to Terry a couple of times - he was just like, "Dude, you REALLY don't want to be able to feel anything AT ALL down there right now - trust me..."

While everyone busied themselves around me, attaching me to more drips and monitors (I mean, it felt like there were dozens - I think there was just the one drip, though...), and doing God knows what else, the anaesthetist started to do more tests to make sure the spinal block had worked properly. This involved her basically spraying my body with cold water, and asking me to tell her when I could feel the coldness of it. This was actually surprisingly tricky, because she'd told me I would always feel the water itself - it was the temperature she wanted to know about, and, me being me, I got a bit panicky about this, and kept worrying about getting the "wrong" answer. A lot of the time I just couldn't work out whether what I was feeling was cold or not, so it was a bit like when you go to the opticians, and they're all, "Is it better with this lens, or with this one?" and you become quietly convinced that they're not actually changing the lenses at all, but are just trying to catch you out.

Or is that just me?

Anyway, because of my dithering over whether the water I was feeling was cold or maybe just lukewarm, I suspect this part took a bit longer than it really needed to, but soon enough the anaesthetist declared herself satisfied, and we were ready to start - or I assume so: I wasn't actually told when they'd begun the procedure, which is how I'd wanted it to go - I couldn't feel anything at all, other than my body occasionally being moved around, but then, after a few seconds, I started feeling really nauseous, which panicked me a bit, because I was lying on my back, and I really didn't want to throw up. (Or I would choke to death, obviously.) Luckily, though, as soon as I mentioned this to the midwife (Who was at the opposite shoulder from Terry), she sprang into action. "We're on it!" she told me cheerfully, then they added something to the drip, and instantly - INSTANTLY - the nausea disappeared. Wish I'd had whatever that was during the 1st trimester, that's all I'm saying...

The nausea may have gone, however, but now I had another issue: THE SHAKING.

I just could not stop shaking.

I'm not sure if it was from the cold (I'm told the operating theatre is always freezing, although I wasn't actually aware of it), the anxiety, or, well, THE DRUGS, but both arms started shaking uncontrollably, and I just couldn't make it stop. I remember all I could say for the first part of the procedure was, "I can't stop shaking! I can't stop shaking!" I said this so often I think I freaked Terry out a bit, as he had no idea what to do to help me: I was (stupidly) worried they wouldn't be able to go ahead with the surgery if I couldn't stop myself shaking, but, of course, my lower body was completely still - and, unbeknown to me, they were almost done at that point anyway. In every c-section story I've read, the woman writing it has said how quickly it went: to me, it actually felt like it took a really long time. I remember asking Terry if there was something wrong, because it seemed to be taking so long. "Would they all be chatting and laughing if there was something wrong?" he asked, and sure enough, although I couldn't focus on what they were saying, I could tell that the surgical team were all chatting away, almost as if they *weren't* just about to pull a live human from my body, so that was comforting...

"I know you don't want to be told what's happening," the midwife said suddenly, around 10- 15 minutes in, "But there's a bit coming up that you need to be prepared for..."

At this, the surgeon stuck her head over the curtain.

"That part's coming up right now," she said, cheerfully. "Brace yourself!"

The next second, I felt a huge pressure bearing down on my chest. I'm not going to lie - it was absolutely terrifying: even more so because it wasn't something I'd read about in any of the many, many c-section birth stories I'd read, so I totally wasn't expecting it. The pressure continued, though, and I started crying - not in pain, really, just in sheer terror: at one point I remember thinking, "They obviously don't realise how hard they're pushing down, but they're going to break my ribs if they don't stop..." Pretty freaky, really.

"I can't breathe!" I sobbed, dramatically. "I can't breathe!" (I totally could breathe, by the way: I was just panicking...) "I really can't do this!"

And then, all of a sudden, a baby started crying.

Loudly.

Oh. My. God.

On the way down to theatre, the midwife had warned me that c-section babies don't always cry when they're born, and that I shouldn't panic if he didn't. Max, however, came into the world - to the strains of Uptown Funk, incidentally - screaming. And it was the best sound I've ever heard - or ever WILL hear - in my life.

"Congratulations!" said the surgeon, peering over the curtain. "He's absolutely gorgeous!"

I couldn't reply though, because as soon as that cry rang out, I started SOBBING - these giant, uncontrollable sobs of relief that he was here, and he was - judging from what I could hear - safe. It was the best feeling in the world: I totally forgot about my shaking arms, and the fact that my body was presumably open to the elements at that point: I just lay there and sobbed, until the surgical team all started laughing, and telling me to stop making them so emotional.

Our hospital does delayed cord clamping, so there was no dramatic, "baby being lifted over the curtain moment," which I was a little bit disappointed about.

"Look at all that hair!" I heard someone say, so I asked Terry if he wanted to take a look.

"Does he look like you?" I asked him. Terry, however, was also in tears at this point, so he just stood up slightly and took a quick look over the curtain.

"He has black hair," he managed to say through his tears, as he sat back down, and then we both cried a bit more as we waited to meet our little boy. I think this was probably the hardest part of the whole thing, and probably the biggest downside to having a c-section: as soon as he was born, I just wanted to hold him, but while it only took a few minutes for them to finish cutting the cord (They cut it long, then offer the father the opportunity to cut it shorter afterwards: Terry wasn't bothered about that, though...), it felt like forever.

A few minutes later, though, the midwife appeared at my side again, clutching the most precious little bundle ever:

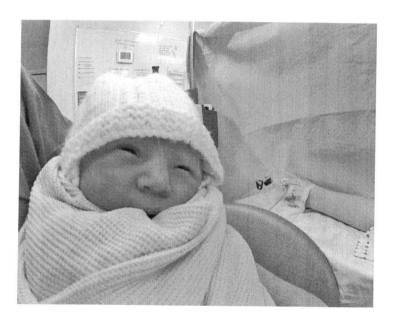

Max's face all was squashed from being in the womb (He

changed so much just in the first couple of days!) and bright red from crying (He also had a touch of jaundice when he was born, which cleared up on its own), but he was hands down the most beautiful thing I'd ever seen. There wasn't enough room for him to lie on my chest, but the midwife held him next to me, and I was able to reach out and stroke his soft little cheek, before he was whisked off to recovery to be cleaned, weighed and checked over. Terry went with him (He had offered to stay with me, but I wanted him to go with the baby), and I endured the longest few minutes of my life while they were gone: I'd stopped shaking now, and I honestly couldn't have cared less what was happening on the other side of the curtain - all I could think about was my beautiful baby boy, and how I just couldn't believe he was actually here. A nurse took Terry's seat while he was gone, to keep an eye on me: I think she was chatting to me about New Year's Eve, or Christmas, or something, but I honestly can't remember, I was just so focused on the baby, and when I'd get to see him again. This part also seemed to take forever, but it was really just a couple of minutes before a beaming Terry re-appeared, with that precious little bundle in his arms:

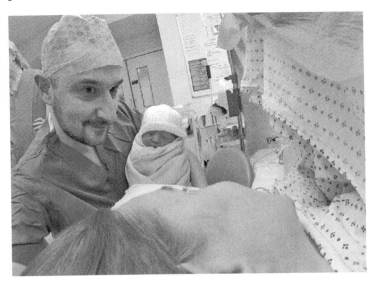

I can't even describe how it felt to finally see him, after all this time. People had warned me that I might not feel that rush of love everyone talks about, and that it can sometimes take time, but I'd loved him before he was born, and he was so exactly as I'd imagined him (Throughout my pregnancy, people kept fixating on the idea of me having a "ginger" baby - to an extent that actually became quite upsetting, if I'm honest - but I'd always imagined a little black haired boy, just like his daddy...) that I just couldn't stop crying, and smiling, and staring at him.

Meanwhile, of course, the surgical team were busy sewing me back up, and soon enough the midwife came to take Terry back to the room we'd been in earlier, to change back into his own clothes. While he was gone, the baby was placed in the incubator, and I was moved from the operating table to a bed (All I'll say here is that it took every person present to lift me...) and wheeled into the recovery room next door. By this point, I still hadn't held the baby, and it was all I could think about: I'd asked to do skin-to-skin as soon as possible, so once they'd wheeled us both into recovery, the nurses helped me pull my gown down, and one of them picked up Max and laid him on my chest.

He'd started crying as soon as he was picked up, but the second he touched me, he stopped, and just stared up at me with his big, dark blue eyes.

And there he was.

There were the little fists I'd felt hammering away at my belly all those months.

There was the tiny nose I'd seen so many times on the ultrasound, and the little chubby cheeks.

He was simultaneously so familiar, and so totally brand new, that holding him for the first time was absolutely magical - especially when he immediately cuddled in to my chest, and lay there contentedly. After a few minutes, Terry joined us for more Staring in Amazement: we were both just so emotional at this point that we could barely speak, and I don't even remember what we said. I'm going to guess it was just endless variations of, "Can you BELIEVE he's here?" and "We MADE him!" though, because that's pretty much all we said for the first few hours.

I'm not sure how long I was in recovery, but it seemed pretty quick, and the next thing I knew, I was being wheeled up to the ward, still with my top pulled down and the baby snuggled against me. Once again, I was taken through the public part of the hospital - I remember going past the front door of the Labour and Delivery suite, plus the crowded waiting room I'd sat in a few times while I was still pregnant. Ordinarily, I'd have been mortified to be seen like that, but I was just so elated they could have wheeled me naked through the centre of town, and I honestly wouldn't have cared.

(OK, I totally would have. Glad that didn't happen.)

Throughout my pregnancy, I hadn't ever allowed myself to feel excited - I just hadn't dared. As they wheeled me up to the ward, though, it was like 9 months worth of stored-up excitement arrived at once, as I finally allowed myself to believe that we were actually going to be allowed to do this: I really would get to see my baby boy in the beautiful nursery we'd created for him; I'd get to dress him in all of those little outfits that were hanging up in his closet, and do all of the things we hadn't even dared to plan. By the time we reached my room, I had allowed myself to imagine it all: the birthdays and the Christmases; the holidays and school days, and everything in between. I'd left this room less than two hours before: but in the time I'd been gone, the whole world had changed. Two of has had walked down to theatre, but three had come back - and three we would be, from now on.

There was one more thing I'd been looking forward to since before I was even pregnant, though, and I finally got to see it happen just an hour or so after Max was born, when my parents arrived to meet their new grandson for the first time:

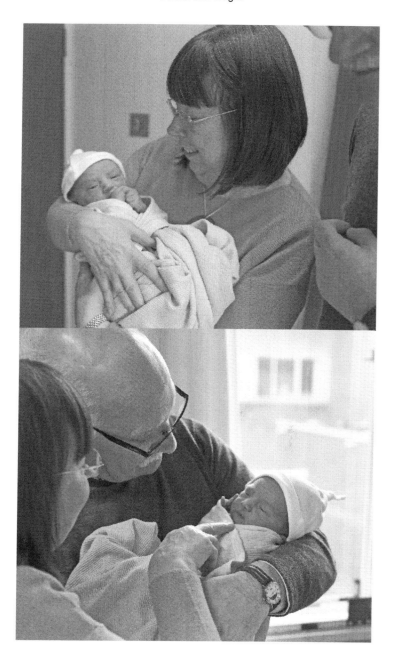

And then there was this...

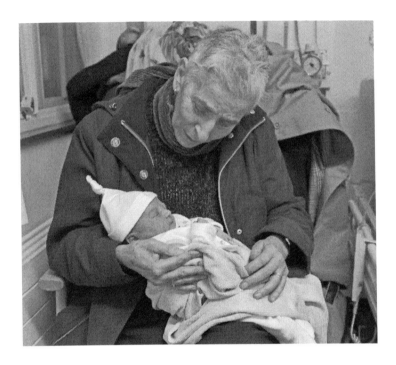

Terry's mum meeting Max: a moment we'd been told might not happen, and which, at times, had seemed so unlikely as to be totally impossible. And yet, here she was: and here *he* was, too. It was a day of impossible things: of firsts and lasts, and memories that will stay with us for the rest of our lives. Our little boy, surrounded by the people who love him most - and who we love most in return. And it would never happen again, quite like this: as I lay on my hospital bed, legs still tingling from the spinal block, I knew this moment was precious: that it was the very first time we'd all been together like this, but that it would likely be the last time, too.
And so it was.

Two days after this photo was taken, Terry's mum was admitted to hospice care in Edinburgh. She passed peacefully away on January 28th, 2018, having confounded her doctor's expectations, to survive one month longer than the six months she was given, way back in June. She'd been determined to meet her newest grandchild, and, in true, Soula style, she was as good as her word - and then some.

So, beginnings and endings, befores and afters, the highest of highs, and the very lowest of lows, all combined to make up the longest, shortest, happiest, saddest, hardest and most life-changing year of our lives. And you want to know the scariest, and most wonderful thing of all?

We were only just getting started.

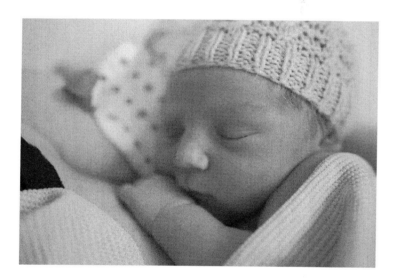

Our story continues at

www.ForeverAmber.co.uk

and on Instgram @foreveramberblog

Printed in Great Britain
by Amazon